Also by Kimberly M. Hanlon

The Minnesota Cabin Planning Guide & Workbook

THE MINNESOTA SMALL BUSINESS OWNER'S LEGAL SURVIVAL GUIDE

(HOW TO AVOID THE 15 LEGAL SNARES THAT CAN RUIN YOUR BUSINESS, TAKE OVER YOUR LIFE, AND LEAVE YOU BANKRUPT.)

BY KIMBERLY M. HANLON

The Minnesota Small Business Owner's Legal Survival Guide

Published by
Propitious Publishing, Inc.
310 4th Avenue South
Suite 5010
Minneapolis, Minnesota 55415

ISBN: 9780985933739 (PDF)
ISBN: 9780985933746 (Kindle)
ISBN: 9780985933753 (Paperback)

PROPITIOUS
— PUBLISHING INC. —

To my wonderful husband, Richard. Thank you for graciously keeping our home and lives running smoothly as I while away the hours working, working, working. Or said another way, doing what I like to do best. I love you.

Acknowledgements

I have so much to be grateful for, and for nothing more than the people in my life who give me the support to go out and conquer the world. First of all, my parents who have not only been the source of life for me, but who continue to be the most wonderful comrades in arms through life with me. In the context of this book, thank you to my mom, Sara, for encouraging me to bring yet another "hair brained scheme" into fruition. In the context of this book, thank you to my dad, Bill, for being so committed to editing this book and making it much better than it would have been without you. Second, my wonderful husband Richard who has been God's unexpected gift to me. In the context of this book, thank you for never complaining as I stayed up late, typing away, instead of coming to bed. Third, to my law partner, Sommer, who has become my favorite partner-in-crime. In the context of this book, thank you for picking up our workload and doing the heavy lifting while I got the book finished. I could not be more lucky and blessed than to have you by my side, building our firm and a whole new model for practicing law.

Table of Contents

Introduction

Over the years, I've noticed that people go into business for themselves because they are very good technicians in their field of work, and either they believe they can make more money if they work for themselves, or they will have more time or flexibility for other commitments, or they will enjoy life more if they aren't under the watchful eye of a boss. Whatever the motivating reason to have a business of their own, without fail every business owner discovers that they need to know much, much more than their technical field of expertise if they are going to succeed.

When it comes to business, ignorance isn't bliss; ignorance is risk. There's a handful of legal topics that business owners should be familiar with, at least on a rudimentary level, to reduce the risk of having something horrible come out of left field. That's what this book is about. My intention in arming you with information is so that you can proceed in business confidently and with fewer legal quagmires.

Each of these chapters is a subject that could be the topic of its own book, or even encyclopedia set of books. If you wanted that level of detail you would have gone to law school instead of starting a business. I promise I won't bore you with every nuanced detail of every aspect of the law. That said, keep in mind that the law is in fact quite detailed and nuanced.

This book is a legal guide to help you put the most common business legal issues on your radar, with enough information for you to be on alert for when you may need to get some professional advice. As the disclaimer at the inside of the title page states, this book is not intended as legal advice and you should seek the advice of a lawyer for any particular situation that arises as it applies to you.

Chapter 1: Which entity is best for my business? (a guide to LLCs, corporations, and more)

Would you rather have every penny you have and every asset you own to be up for grabs if something goes wrong with your business? Or would you rather have a limited amount of your money and none of your personal assets be up for grabs? I'm guessing you would rather have the limited risk; I know that's my first choice in my business.

At its core, that is what setting up a business entity is all about. Of course, there are various tax benefits as well. If you want to get the inside scoop on making business entities work for you, read on.

a.   Do I have to have a corporation or LLC?

According to the Small Business Administration, over 70% of businesses in the U.S. are sole proprietorships, meaning they have no separate corporate entity structure independent of its owner. Why would that be, if there are so many benefits to having a business entity like a corporation or an LLC? It's because a sole proprietorship (or its multi-member twin, the general partnership) is the default setting for a business. If you don't actively set up another business entity type, you are automatically classified as a sole proprietorship (or general partnership, if there's more than one of you).

With all those sole proprietorships, clearly you don't actually have to have a corporation or an LLC. No one is going to come by and force you to set up a business entity. The question, though, is, should you?

b. If you do nothing: sole proprietorships and general partnerships

What do business entities like corporations and LLC's have that sole proprietorships and general partnerships don't have? For one, personal asset protection. Here's how it works: when you are an owner of a sole proprietorship or general partnership, everything you do with your business is an extension of you as a person. Your business finances are an extension of your personal finances, meaning you are personally liable for all the debts of your business.

At this point, you may be thinking "but my business doesn't have any debts," and you might be right. But if someone brought a lawsuit against your business (which is against you because your business is an extension of you as a person) and won, the judgment that results is a type of debt. Now your business has debt, and so do you.

If you don't pay that debt, the creditor can levy your accounts and put a lien on your house. If you have real estate other than your home, like a family cabin or a rental property, the creditor can put a lien on that property and force a foreclosure because your non-homestead property isn't protected by homestead exemptions.

If worst comes to worst, the creditor can get the sheriff to gather your non-exempt assets and sell them at auction (for pennies on the dollar) to apply towards the debt. Imagine – the sheriff collects $25,000 of your personal stuff to pay off $10,000 worth of business debt.

i. Sole proprietorships

If you are one person who has started a business without any other partners and you haven't done anything to register your business as a particular type of a business entity, then your business is a sole proprietorship. That is why sole proprietorships make up the vast majority of businesses in the U.S.

If you have a sole proprietorship that is doing business by a name other than your personal name then you will need to register the business name as a "doing business as" or "DBA" or" Assumed Name" with the states in which you do business.

As we talked about earlier, sole proprietorships come with significant risks for owner's personal assets. But, that's not all. When you are a sole proprietorship, your business expenses go on your personal tax return on a Schedule C. And that increases your odds of being audited by the IRS. Why? Because the IRS knows that sole proprietorships can have blurry lines as to what the real expenses were regarding travel, meals and entertainment, and home office expenses, among others. If you really want to increase your odds of being audited, be a sole proprietorship with questionable tax entries.

ii. General partnerships

A general partnership is formed when two people or more start to carry on a business for profit. If those people don't form some other kind of business entity, then the business will continue to be a general partnership until they do. When it comes to general partnerships, each partner is fully responsible and liable for the actions of every other partner. If one partner does something wrong, either by accident or on purpose, everybody pays.

A general partnership is a separate and distinct entity apart from its owners, but the owners remain personally liable for all the debts of the business. The partnership owns property separate from the owners and that property is not considered the property of the partners, even though the partners are personally responsible for the debts that arise from the property.

Under the default partnership rules, each partner has an equal vote in the management of the business and an equal share of the profit distributions. Partners can choose to alter the default rules, with some limitations, by creating a Partnership Agreement.

For tax purposes, the partnership itself files a tax return and each partner is given a K-1 statement that details that partner's share of tax liability to be reported on that partner's personal tax return.

c. The corporation variety pack: C's, S's, and B's

Corporations are legal entities that exist as their own legal "person", separate from you. Because they are their own separate legal "person" from you, they are not an extension of you personally, provided that you set up and manage it correctly (the "corporate formalities"). Since the corporation is not an extension of you, any debts and liabilities of the corporation stop there and don't impact your personal accounts and assets.

All corporations, no matter what type, require articles of incorporation, bylaws, an annual meeting of shareholders, an annual meeting of directors, and maintenance of the corporate records at a minimum to observe the "corporate formalities" that prevent someone from piercing the corporate veil, which would make the shareholders personally liable as though it were a sole proprietorship or general partnership.

The difference between a C-corp and S-corp has to do with how the taxes are handled, and B-corp has to do with the ability to put a portion of profits to a beneficial social purpose.

i. C-corporations

C-corporations were the first type of corporation to be developed by the law, and are still the default type of corporation that gets set up. If you want your business to be taxed as an S-corporation, you must make an election to be taxed that way.

C-corps pay a corporate income tax on its profits, and then shareholders (owners) pay personal income tax on the salaries they get paid for working for the company and on the profit distributions they get as owners of the company. That's why people talk about C-corps having double taxation; the company pays taxes and then the owners pay taxes again.

Have you ever heard the term "fringe benefits?" C-corp fringe benefits allow the company to pay owner-employee health benefits, vehicle expenses, life insurance plans, long-term care plans, and certain education expenses tax free to the owners. They also have more retirement planning options than other types of entities. That sounds great, right? Right! But consider this – the company has to have a lot of cash to pay for all those benefits. If your company doesn't have a lot of money in which to pay for those benefits, you're not really going to be able to benefit from them.

If a C-corp decides to keep a portion of its profits and reinvest them in the company (called retained earnings), then the owners don't pay income tax on that amount. A business cannot retain earnings solely for the purpose of avoiding owner's income tax; if it does then the IRS has special taxes that will apply.

Publicly held companies are C-corps, and this business structure is the best to use for privately held companies when there will be frequent changes in stock ownership.

   ii.   S-corporations

S-corporations were formed to allow small businesses to be taxed more like a sole proprietorship or general partnership but have the asset protection and other benefits of being a corporation. With an S-corp, the profits from the business "pass through" to the owners and get taxed on the owner's personal tax return under their personal income tax rate. If the owners of an S-corp keep some of the business' profits in the company (like retained earnings), they still pay personal income taxes on that amount, even though they didn't actually take that money home.

The rules about who can be an S-corp shareholder are rather strict. You must be a US citizen or resident alien ("green card holder") and if it is a trust or business entity, it only qualifies if the trust or business entity is solely owned by the individual in a "pass through" capacity (i.e. single member LLCs, revocable grantor trusts). If that last bit seems confusing, that's because it is. Here's the bottom line: if you are a person who is a US citizen or resident alien, you're good to go. Anything else, ask your lawyer. An S-corp can only have up to 100 shareholders, and any more than that then it has to be a C-corp.

Some small business owners like S-corps because they can take a portion of their proceeds from the business as salary (taxed as earned income) and a portion as dividends (taxed at the lower investment income rate). When business owners do this, it is important to make sure that the salary is not unreasonably low, or else Uncle Sam will have something to say about it.

iii.   B-corporations

Under the traditional corporation rules, the board of directors and the executives of the business have a duty to maximize profits for shareholders. Recently, business founders have wanted to create for-profit businesses that allocate a certain amount of profits towards some socially beneficial purpose. As long as all shareholders agreed with that plan, there wouldn't be a problem. But as soon as a shareholder wasn't on board with allocating a portion of profits to the social purpose, a shareholder lawsuit could be brought against the board and executive team for failing in its duty to the shareholders.

B-corporations are the new corporation type that allow the founders to state a particular beneficial social purpose that a portion of profits can be allocated towards without violating the duty to maximize profits for shareholders. For people who are interested in doing some good with their for-profit business, and don't want to start a non-profit organization, a B-corp may be the perfect solution.

Some well-known B-corps include the clothing company Patagonia (which focuses on sustainability and grassroots environmentalism), the ice-cream company Ben & Jerry's (which supports a stunning array of community projects), and soap company Method (which focuses on recycling, reducing water usage and manufacturing, and sustainability, among other things).

B-corporations can choose to be taxed as either a C-corp or as an S-corp. If you're interested in learning more about B-corps, a great website to visit is www.bcorporation.net.

d. All about LLC's

Limited Liability Companies (LLC's) have the asset protection of corporations while having less stringent requirements for keeping corporate formalities, which is why so many business owners like this entity structure. Also, an LLC can elect to be taxed like a sole proprietor (or general partnership), or like an S-corp, or like a C-corp. With an LLC, the owners are called "members", the stock shares are called "units", and the directors on the board are called "governors."

Minnesota recently changed its LLC laws and the new default rules are not what most people expect them to be. The old law was more similar to the rules for corporations and the new law is more similar to the rules for partnerships. Under the new law, a 99% owner and a 1% owner each have an equal vote in making business decisions. Also, a 99% owner and a 1% owner have equal rights to profit distributions. And, owners who put money into the business as capital contributions have to wait until the company is dissolved before getting paid back their contribution.

If this has you saying "what the heck?!?", you're not alone. That's why owners have the opportunity to create different rules from the default rules for their company through an Operating Agreement. There are two potential aspects to an Operating Agreement; the first is detailing the management rules (who gets what voting rights, and distribution rights, and decision-making rights) and the second aspect is the buy-sell provisions we talk about in more depth in Chapter 4 *Playing Nice with Others* (business partner essentials).

LLC's can be managed by the members (owners), managed by a board (board of governors), or by a manager.

From time to time, you may see the designation "PLLC" after a business' name. All this means is that the business is subject to the Professional Firms Act (like doctors, lawyers, accountants, and architects) and have chosen to add the "P" to their "LLC" designation.

e. The smorgasbord of other choices you've never heard of and probably don't need (but let's talk about them briefly, just in case)

The following business structures are not nearly as common, but do serve a purpose in certain circumstances. All of these are types of partnerships, which by its very definition requires more than one person. The important terms about how these businesses operate are created in the Partnership Agreement.

i. Limited Liability Partnerships (LLP's)

Limited Liability Partnerships are similar to limited liability companies in that they protect the owners from the liability of the business. Under the New Minnesota law, LLP's and LLC's are more similar than ever before. However, an LLP can only be taxed as a partnership. LLP's are often used by professional firms like doctors, lawyers, architects, and accountants.

ii. Limited Partnerships (LP's)

Limited Partnerships have at least one general partner who is responsible for managing the business and one limited partner who has no part in managing the business. The general partners have full personal liability for the business just like in a general partnership, but the limited partner has personal asset protection from the liabilities of the business.

iii. Limited Liability Limited Partnerships (LLLP's)

Limited Liability Limited Partnerships combine the structure of a limited partnership with the liability protection for the managing partners like in a limited liability partnership. Nationwide they are relatively rare as not every state recognizes them. We are lucky that Minnesota is one of the states that allows LLLP's.

f. Making the right choice for your business

Making the right choice for your business is a multifaceted decision. We often look at the liability protection from one angle and the tax implications from another angle. There are some parts of planning that make a difference for asset protection but make no difference on the tax bill, and there some parts of planning that make no difference for asset protection but make a huge difference on the tax bill. That's why we often recommend that people work with their attorney and their CPA in tandem when they're making their business formation decisions.

Depending on the nature of your business, sometimes we like to set up more than one entity for strategies with more asset protection and tax advantages. Sometimes it is more than one LLC, or more than one corporation, or a mix of a corporation and an LLC, or limited partnership with a corporation or an LLC as the general partner.

g. Changing your mind later

If you set your business up in one structure and change your mind later, it's not the end of the world and you can change into a new type of entity. That said, some changes are easier to make than others. It is easier to change from an LLC to a corporation from a tax perspective. If you do make a change, there's a time frame in which you have to keep the new structure before you would be allowed to switch back, so it's important to think through the decision before making the change. Oftentimes businesses start small as an LLC and then grow into a business that is better served as a corporation for attracting investors.

Chapter 2: Making it all legal (registering and licensing your business)

a. Minnesota? Delaware? Nevada? Wyoming? (where to register your business and why)

If you live in Minnesota and your business is only going to do business in Minnesota then there's really no advantage to setting your business up in another state. If, however, your business is going to do business in multiple states then there may be a good reason to set up your business in another state. In Minnesota, we have a state corporate tax, individual state income tax, and sales and use tax. If you live here and do business here you are going to be subject to these taxes regardless of what state your business is set up in.

On the other hand, if you do business in multiple states, not every state has a corporate tax or sales and use tax and you may save on some taxes on some portion of the business revenue if you are set up in a different state. Of course, the portion of business that you do in Minnesota will still be subject to all the Minnesota taxes but if you're doing a significant amount of business outside of Minnesota, it may be worthwhile to explore your other options. The most popular choices for other states for business formation are Delaware, Nevada, and Wyoming.

i. Minnesota

For Minnesotans, the benefits for forming a Minnesota based business include an easy to use electronic filing system with the secretary of state, local attorneys familiar with the state's business laws, and free annual renewals if done online and on time. As we mentioned earlier, there isn't a tax savings for a Minnesota owner who does business only in Minnesota so for most business owners the benefits of forming the business in Minnesota outweighs the expense and hassle of forming in another state.

If you do form your business in another state but are going to do business in Minnesota, you'll need to register your business as a foreign business doing business in Minnesota.

ii. Delaware

The common perception is that Delaware is the best state to organize your business in, but that is not always the case. Delaware laws are geared towards large public corporations and the courts and case law tend to favor management over minority shareholders and that's why many Fortune 500 companies favor Delaware. If you're going to grow your business into a Fortune 500 company, then you might want to consider Delaware.

Delaware does have a state corporate income tax, personal state income tax, and a state franchise tax, so this is not the place to turn for tax savings.

iii. Nevada

Nevada is always on the list of states that are good for business because Nevada has no state corporate income tax and no state personal income tax. However, if you have one or more businesses in Nevada and the cumulative gross income of those businesses is over four million dollars, you will be subject to Nevada's commerce tax. Nevada has expensive formation and annual renewal fees that are much higher than Minnesota's.

Nevada is known for having the best protection for owners from having the corporate veil be pierced. It is also the only state that does not share information with the IRS. Of course, that can make you a target of the IRS since they're not getting your business information from the state.

iv. Wyoming

Wyoming is generally considered a good state for small businesses. Like Nevada, it has no state corporate income tax and no personal income tax, and provides good protection for owners from having the corporate veil pierced. Unlike Nevada, Wyoming has minimal initial setup and annual fees. If you're looking for a good state to set up a business in, you should consider Wyoming.

b. Licensing for particular industries

For the vast majority of business owners, they set up their business and are able to start serving the public. For people in specific industries, however, additional licensing at the state, county, or city level may be required. For the most part these licensing requirements are intended to protect the public.

We're not going to list every possible licensing requirement in this book. For one thing, the requirements are often changing. For another, the list would simply be too long. Instead, go to the state's central repository for business licensing at www.mn.gov/elicense/.

c. Federal and State tax registrations

If your business is a sole proprietorship then your personal Social Security number is the business' tax ID as well. Every other type of business needs to have its own tax ID. Single member LLC's can technically get away with using the owner's tax ID as the business' ID, but I think that's a bad idea. Often in the usual course of business the company's tax ID gets shared with vendors and customers so having that ID as your Social Security number increases your personal risk of identity theft.

i. Federal Tax ID

To get a Federal tax ID, otherwise known as a Federal Employer Identification Number (FEIN), go to the IRS web site at www.IRS.gov and enter "FEIN application" in the search box. The application process is free and easy to do. When you get to the end of the process and you'll be asked if you want to receive your number by mail or if you want to receive it immediately by PDF. If you choose the PDF option, your tax ID letter will appear on the screen and that will be your one and only opportunity to save that letter. So as soon as that letter opens, download it onto your computer!

ii.   State Tax ID

If you're doing business in states other than Minnesota, you'll need to research and comply with those states' tax regulations and reporting requirements. If you're doing business in Minnesota, you can apply for your state business tax ID at www.revenue.state.mn.us/businesses/.

d.   Annual renewals and other maintenance requirements

You don't want to let your business registration lapse because you'll lose the asset protection aspect of your entity during that lapse. If you have forgotten to stay on top of your business registration it's important that you get it current before something happens.

If you have registered your business with the state of Minnesota, the good news is that you can do your annual renewal for free if you do it online and on time. If you don't do it on time, you can still do your renewal online but you'll pay a fee to get your registration up to date. To renew online, go to the Minnesota Secretary of state's web site at www.sos.state.mn.us/business-liens. I suggest you make a calendar entry each year shortly before the new year so you don't forget.

If you have registered your business in another state, you'll need to stay on top of your annual renewal using their system.

Corporations of all types are required to have an annual meeting of shareholders and an annual meeting of directors, which in a small business are often the same people in the same meeting. It is important to memorialize that meeting in writing even if there's only one shareholder or director. While LLC's are not required to have this annual meeting, it is still a good idea for the LLC members to have an annual meeting and memorialize it in writing.

The more things LLC owners can do that reflect "corporate formalities" the stronger the asset protection the LLC will have. I recommend having the annual meeting around the same time as the renewal so it doesn't get forgotten, or at least have the memorialization of the meeting at that time.

Chapter 3: The un-shirkable duties (the legal obligations and duties of those running the show)

When more than one person owns a business, each business owner has certain duties to their fellow owners. Likewise, when someone is running a business and making important business decisions, they owe those duties to the people who own the business. It makes sense, right? You wouldn't want someone making business decisions that were against the business' interest behind your back.

In a partnership, corporation, or LLC, the people who are making business decisions have certain duties that they owe to the company and the owners under the law. To a certain extent, these duties can be curtailed by agreement of all the owners. For the most part, though, these are the duties that are in operation in most companies.

These duties are articulated slightly differently in the text of the law between partnerships and corporations and LLC's. Without getting too technical, here's an overview of those duties.

a. The Fiduciary Duties

The general duties that directors and officers owe to the business owners, and owners to each other, are generally acting in good faith, in a way that is in the business' best interests, and with the care that a reasonable person would give in the same or similar situation. That can be broken down further into two specific duties, the duty of loyalty and the duty of care.

i. Duty of Loyalty

The duty of loyalty has a handful of components including the duty to account to the company and to take care of the company's property, profits, and benefits to the owners; to not use the company's property for personal benefit; to not enter into transactions where there's a conflict of interest (where that person is benefiting from the transaction or acting on behalf of someone whose interests are not the same as the company's); and to not compete against the company (which means the person must bring all business opportunities relevant to the company to the company).

A company may allow a transaction that violates the duty of loyalty if all owners agree. For instance, a co-owner can have another business they own serve as a vendor for the company if all of the other owners of that company agreed to it.

In a partnership, partners also have a duty to disclose important facts about the business to each other including the financial state of the business and providing access to the business' books and records.

ii. Duty of Care

At the base of the duty of care is the "business judgment rule." Actions are generally protected by the business judgment rule when the person acts in good faith, on an informed basis, and in the best interest of the business. So, part of the duty of care is getting the information needed to make a good business decision. The more significant the decision, the more important it is to make sure that you have done the proper research before deciding.

In relation to this duty, you have the right to rely on expert advisers unless, of course, you have reason to believe that you shouldn't rely on that advice. The practical effect of the business judgment rule is that the person making the decision won't be liable to the other business owners as long as they acted in good faith, had no conflict of interest, and did reasonable research about the decision even if it turned out to be a bad decision.

Minnesota courts have rarely found decision makers to be liable under the duty of care alone, and usually only do so if there is fraud, collusion, or some other misconduct.

b. Additional duties under the New LLC law

Under the new LLC law, there are additional duties that are listed. These include the obligation of good faith and fair dealing which mean that the person acts in a way that is honest, fair, and reasonable. You may think that this shouldn't need to be stated in law, but it has come up from time to time.

c. Opting out of the usual duties

In a corporation, the monetary liability for a breach of the fiduciary duties can be limited or eliminated in the Articles of Incorporation. When it comes to LLC's and partnerships, the rules aren't so cut and dried.

In a partnership, the partners may make a Partnership Agreement that alters some but not all aspects of the fiduciary duties. First, let's look at what a Partnership Agreement cannot change. It cannot change a partner's right to access the books and records of the business, it cannot eliminate the duty of loyalty, it cannot eliminate the obligation of good faith and fair dealing, and it cannot unreasonably reduce the duty of care. It can, however, allow the partners to specify types of activities that would not violate the duty of loyalty provided that those things are not obviously unreasonable, and they can state standards of performance to measure the obligation of good faith and fair dealing provided that those standards are not obviously unreasonable.

In a Limited Partnership, the general partner owes full fiduciary duties to the limited partners, but the duty of care that limited partners owe is limited to refraining from engaging in grossly negligent or reckless conduct, intentional misconduct, or knowingly breaking the law.

In an LLC, similarly to a partnership, the owners may make an Operating Agreement that alters some but not all aspects of the fiduciary duties. The Operating Agreement may not eliminate the duty of loyalty, the duty of care, or any other fiduciary duty, or eliminate the obligation of good faith and fair dealing. It also may not restrict the owners' access to information and records about the business. The operating agreement can, however, restrict or eliminate the specific duty to not use the company's property for personal benefit, to not enter into transactions where there's a conflict of interest, and to not compete against the company.

Also similar to a partnership, owners may specify types of activities that would not violate the duty of loyalty, they may alter the duty of care except for authorizing intentional misconduct or knowingly breaking the law, and they may alter any other fiduciary duty including eliminating particular aspects of that duty in the Operating Agreement. They may also state standards of performance to measure the obligation of good faith and fair dealing. All of these changes must not be obviously unreasonable, of course.

When an LLC has voting members and nonvoting members, it is similar to a Limited Partnership that has general partners running the show and limited partners with no management rights. Similarly, an LLC can eliminate fiduciary duties for those nonvoting members when their responsibility for making decisions has been eliminated in the Operating Agreement.

d.   What to do if a co-owner is breaching a duty

If you're in business with someone else and there is a breach of fiduciary duty, it is a breach of trust. Usually a breach of fiduciary duty results in a financial loss. Some examples of breaches include:

- A business partner taking a business opportunity away from the company for his or her own benefit
- A business partner taking an action against the interests of the company for his or her own financial gain
- A business partner keeping a portion of the profits that he or she is not entitled to
- A business partner being negligent in management

- A business partner misrepresenting or hiding relevant information about the business that results in financial loss

If the breach results in financial loss to the company or you, then you have the right to pursue a claim for damages in court. The remedy may include many damages and it may include having that person removed from the business. The person filing the claim has the burden of proof to show the breach, and then the business partner may counter by showing they acted within the bounds of the fiduciary duty.

Chapter 4: Playing nice with others (business partner essentials)

Going into business with somebody else is like a marriage; a business marriage. At the start, everyone is optimistic and willing to overlook all sorts of personal failings. Over time, the happy veneer wears thin as personalities clash during challenges that are inevitable in any business endeavor. That's when the true test of the business relationship happens and that's when the partnership will either make it or break it.

a. The cocktail napkin (the unintended consequences of sharing your business in conversation)

Have you ever sat in a bar or restaurant with a friend or family member and enthusiastically shared your business idea, drawing it all out on a cocktail napkin? And have you ever had that person say, "what a great idea, I'd like to do that with you"? Depending on what you said next, you may or may not have formed a business relationship (whether you meant to or not). If you said something like, "um, well, maybe, okay, I suppose", then there may be some expectation in the other person's mind that they're in business with you, while you thought you were being polite but non-committal.

Then, when they offer helpful advice and contribute good ideas, they think they're helping launch their business while you think they are just being a supportive friend or family member. And then when it comes time for the financial benefits of the business to be divvied up, they expect their share and don't understand why you don't think they are entitled to it as a partner. And then there's a lawsuit. While it may sound farfetched, it happens more often than you might think.

If you happen to be sharing your business idea in conversation and someone is intrigued by the idea and indicates some interest in participating with you, it is best to state clearly that you'll consider it as an option and you'll get back with them with some terms in writing, but that there will be no business partnership until it is agreed to and put down on paper (and I don't mean a cocktail napkin).

b. Why your business needs a Pre-nup and a Will

Okay, your business won't actually have a Pre-nup and it won't actually have a Will, but the same set of planning that people do for a Pre-nup and a Will that benefits their lives as individuals will benefit your business. The business' Pre-nup and Will provisions will be found in the Shareholder Agreement (if a corporation), the Operating Agreement (if an LLC), or the Partnership Agreement (if a partnership). In any of these types of agreements, we call them "buy sell agreements."

These buy sell agreements list certain triggering events (like the death of an owner, for instance), and what happens next after the triggering event. The purpose of the buy sell agreement is to ensure the smooth and continuous operation of the business despite the upset in the status quo. The buy sell agreement is also designed to reduce the likelihood of conflict about the value of the business in cases of buyout. Buy-sell agreements make it possible for co-owners to have some sense of security as to what will happen in specific instances, and if those situations should arise, how they will be handled.

In Minnesota, the court has not taken a generous view towards shareholders wanting to skirt the provisions of the buy-sell agreement when the provisions are clearly stated in writing and properly adopted. It is a good idea to state that all owners agree that the buy-sell agreement incorporates all the expectations of the owners with respect to their interests in the company.

> i. "I think we should just be friends . . ." (what happens if one of you wants (or is forced) out)

Just like in a marriage, it's a good idea to decide what would be fair and equitable in the case of a split while everyone is still happy, optimistic, and thinking that it could never happen to them. Sometimes people go into business together and after a short while it is clear that one partner has a different level of commitment from the other. Or they may discover that they have opposing philosophies about spending money, or risk tolerance, or managing people. Or maybe they discover that their business partner is a cut above the average snake, but a snake nonetheless. When these revelations happen and there isn't a buy sell agreement in place, the conflict that ensues rivals any divorce.

When someone wants out (or their partners want them out), they will want money for their share of the business. If the business were a large public corporation like Coca-Cola, the shareholder could just sell his or her shares to someone else and the other shareholders wouldn't really care. In a small business, though, the other owners do care who those shares are sold to. After all, those owners would be in a business marriage with a buyer without being able to choose their partner.

In the buy sell agreement, we often put in provisions that state that an owner cannot sell his or her shares to an outsider without the consent of every other owner. We also often put in provisions that state that the other owners have the first right to buy those shares instead of the outsider at the same terms negotiated with the outsider. That way, the owners can choose whether they like the outsider and want to go into business with him or her, or if they'd rather pay for the privilege of choosing not to.

In cases where it is important to the business that the initial owners have a lasting commitment, we often put in a provision that states that an owner who leaves before a certain time frame will have his or her buyout at a significant discount.

    ii.   'Til death do us part (and then what?)

When a business owner dies, their shares in the business pass to their heirs according to their estate plan or according to the state's intestacy laws if they haven't planned. So, often a business owners shares are passing to their surviving spouse or their children. Do you want to be business partners with your business partner's spouse or kids? If the answer is no (or even maybe), then your buy sell agreement needs to have provisions for the death of an owner.

If you are certain that you would not want to have your business partner's spouse or kids as a business partner, then your buy sell agreement would state that the remaining owners or the company itself must buy out the deceased partner's share. If you're open to the possibility of having your business partner's spouse or kids as a business partner but want to decide later, then your buy sell agreement would state that the remaining owners or the company itself has the first right to choose whether or not to buy back the deceased partner's share.

iii. When one can no longer carry the buckets (making provisions for permanent disability)

According to the social security Administration, one in four 20-year-olds will become permanently disabled before they reach retirement age. That means disability planning is an important aspect in any buy sell agreement. When a business partner becomes disabled, even partially disabled, the workload and decision-making they were doing can no longer be done by them. However, they are still owners and still entitled to an owner share the profits. A small business can only operate for so long paying out to an owner who isn't able to carry their load.

For business owners who do become disabled, the situation can be bleak. They lose the source of their income at the same time that they have increasing medical costs and little chance to recover physically or financially.

Businesses often purchase disability insurance on the business partners. That insurance can be used to replace the business owner as a worker within the business while they are away, and can be used to buy out their share if they are unable to come back after a specific amount time. Even if a business does not buy disability insurance, the buy sell agreement can be structured to allow for the disabled business owner to be bought out in installments making it affordable for the company to do the buyout while providing some source of income for the disabled partner for some time.

  iv. The insidious ex-spouse (the co-owner you didn't pick)

When a married business owner gets a divorce, the divorce judge may split the shares in the business between the business owner in his or her ex. Then suddenly the ex-spouse is a partner in the business, like it or not.

In the buy sell agreement, we often put in provisions that state that the divorcing business owner has the first right to buy out the shares from his or her ex-spouse, and if the divorcing business owner is unwilling or unable to do so, the remaining business owners or the company itself has the second right to buy out their shares.

  v. Creditors and bankruptcy trustees (more co-owners you didn't pick)

Sometimes business owners get into financial hot water in their personal lives and end up filing for bankruptcy. When that happens, their shares in the business is an asset that the bankruptcy trustee can take possession of during the bankruptcy. Unless there is a buy sell agreement that states otherwise, the bankruptcy trustee steps into the shoes of the bankrupt business owner and has all the rights and decision-making powers of that owner.

In the buy sell agreement, we often put in provisions that state that a business owner's bankruptcy triggers that owner's shares to be bought out by their remaining owners or buy the company itself so as to avoid having the bankruptcy trustee come in with decision-making powers.

c. When it comes time to buy someone out

For all the scenarios we just discussed we talked about buying someone out, but we never talked about how much it would be or how it would happen. Without a buy sell agreement, people could spend a lot of time and money arguing over those things.

i. Valuing the business

With a large publicly traded corporation like Coca-Cola, it is easy to know what your shares are worth. The value is tracked every moment when the market is open for trading and the shares are worth whenever amount buyers are willing to pay for them. All you have to do is google the value of a share of Coca-Cola stock and google tells you what the market says the current value is.

It's not so easy with a small, closely held business. The business has a value but there isn't a frequency of trading that would allow the market to tell you what that value would be. To complicate matters, there are multiple ways that businesses get valued. We talk about this in more detail in chapter 14, section B *Selling your Business*.

In the buy sell agreement, we often put in provisions that state the method that will be used to value the business, the qualifications required of the professionals that value the business, and how many appraisals will be used. These are the provisions that we fall back on if the buyers and sellers cannot agree on a price.

Sometimes business owners want to set a specific value for the shares within the agreement, but I don't ever advise going this route. The IRS may ignore the value set by the agreement, and use fair market value for gift and estate tax purposes. If the agreement sets a fixed price for shares, the seller (which may turn out to be your family) may be forced to sell their shares for that lower amount, but pay taxes on each share at a higher amount. If the set amount is too low, your family will not only receive less than market value in exchange for the shares, they will actually end up losing money on the transaction.

30

ii.   Cash at closing

It isn't always easy for a small business to pay the full buyout amount at once, and even if the business could pay out the cash all at once, doing so would generally cripple most businesses such that they would go under shortly after that. At the same time, the seller wants their cash sooner than later and expects to get paid some lump sum.

In the buy sell agreement, we often put in provisions that state that a certain amount of money will be given to the seller at closing. That amount is specified in advance in the agreement and designed to be an amount that will allow the company to continue operating without being crippled, but also an amount that would be acceptable as a down payment for all but the most unreasonable of sellers. That amount is different from one company to the next and may even change over time as the company grows. It's a good idea for business owners to review these terms in their buy sell agreement every few years to make sure they're still workable for the company's current situation.

iii.   The payment plan

As we hinted at in the previous section, sellers usually would rather get paid in one lump sum without regard to the impact on the company. If there's no buy sell agreement in place, sellers are going to be less motivated to accept payment terms. With a buy sell agreement in place, sellers have no choice but to accept those payment terms.

We often state in the buy sell agreement that a sale under a certain amount (the same amount as the closing cash) requires one lump sum payment and anything over that is paid in equal monthly payments over a specific span of time. The span of time indicated in the agreement varies from one company to the next and may change over time as the company grows. Just like in the previous section, this is one area of the buy sell agreement that should be reviewed every few years.

Chapter 5: It's all in the name . . .
(creating and protecting your branding and
intellectual property)

You may not realize it, but pretty much every business has some intellectual property. In some businesses, most of the business' value is in its intellectual property. Even if your business doesn't have a widely recognized logo or trade name, it may still have intellectual property worth protecting.

a.   What is "intellectual property", anyway?

Intellectual property rights can be hard to understand at first because they are assets of the business that you can't actually touch; they aren't physical, they are the product of creativity and thinking. Even if you have an invention, it's the idea that's protected and not the physical gizmo itself.

Examples of intellectual property are artwork and designs, written works, music, symbols and names used in business, architectural work, computer software, manufacturing processes, business plans, client lists, ingredients, systems, sales methods, and the right of publicity.

Intellectual property protection comes in four varieties: patents, trademarks, copyrights, and trade secrets.

i.   The patently obvious (how to protect inventions)

In the U.S., the United States patent and trademark office (USPTO) issues patents that grant exclusive use of an invention throughout the United States, which prevents others from making, using, offering for sale, or selling that invention throughout United States or importing that invention into the United States for a specific amount of time. While everyone associates patents with gizmos, you can get a patent on so many more things. For instance, you can patent processes, machines, business methods, Internet innovations, games, plants, and even odors.

There are three kinds of patents available:

- Utility patents: used for processes, machines, things that get manufactured, and compositions from nature that are made from isolated and extracted natural components (like pharmaceuticals), and protects how the invention works for 20 years
- Design patents: new and original designs of the invention, and protects how the invention looks for 14 years
- Plant patents: newly discovered or created plant varieties that reproduce asexually, like Honeycrisp apples (patented by The University of Minnesota, and which patent recently expired) or roundup ready soybeans (patented by Monsanto, and which patent also recently expired), which protects the seeds for 20 years

You may have heard of a provisional patent, which is a temporary patent that is issued on a shorter application process that must have the full application be completed within a year. If you use the provisional patent process and don't complete the full application within the year, then you lose your ability to complete the patent process and you cannot get a patent on that invention. Some people want to do the provisional patent process to secure protection as quickly as possible but it can be risky because if you're not ready to move forward with a full application on time, then you're out of luck. Full patent applications are not generally quick or easy to complete, so it very well may take longer than a year to get it ready. If you are going to use a provisional patent, it is a good idea to make sure you have sufficient funding to pay for the full application process in time and even possibly have begun some of the documentation and technical drawing work that is so time consuming.

A patent protects the invention in the literal scope of the patent application, as well as from other inventions that may infringe on a patent because they have elements that are identical or equivalent to each claimed element of the patented invention under what we call "the doctrine of equivalents." When considering the functionality test under this doctrine, we ask, "Does the similar invention have a structure that performs substantially the same function and in substantially the same way to achieve substantially the same result?" People often have the misconception that you can change a certain percentage of the design and it will no longer be infringing on a patent, and that may or may not be true, because of the doctrine of equivalents.

Determining if your invention is different enough lies in the claims of the original patent and the claims of your invention. If your invention includes all the claims of the original patent (even if it has additional claims) it is likely infringing on the other patent. Attorneys carefully read patent applications because the exact words from the claims and the technical specifications of the invention matter.

If your invention doesn't infringe on the claims of a current patent, then you can create something that is derived from that original invention and be in the clear. You are free to base your idea on somebody else's patented invention as long as their patent doesn't cover your claims. This is why technology companies spend hours with their patent attorneys and engineers working together to make sure that what they're creating doesn't infringe on their competitors' patents.

As a general rule, it is very expensive to apply for patent protection. The application has to be very carefully drafted with accompanying technical drawings in most cases. Only registered patent attorneys and patent agents can help the public apply for patents, but patent agents cannot provide opinions regarding potential patent infringement because that would be practicing law. To be a patent attorney, the lawyer must also have a technical background (often in engineering, chemistry, or medicine) and they must have the technical or scientific knowledge to understand the client's invention.

Some people only file for patent protection in the United States, while others want to extend their protection globally. In the United States, it is a good idea to get a non-disclosure agreement (a.k.a. NDA) executed with anyone that you're sharing your idea with prior to patent filing, but it will not kill your patent application out of hand if you don't use an NDA as long as your patent application is made within one year of your first unprotected disclosure. If you're going to apply for patent protection outside of the United States, on the other hand, you must use an NDA. Almost every other nation has the policy that any unprotected disclosure makes that invention a donation to the public.

If you are going to apply for a patent, it is important to include every person who was a part of conceiving the invention as a co-inventor. The thing that makes someone a co-inventor is in the conception of the ideas that lead to or become a part of the final product. If someone is simply part of reducing the idea to practice through ordinary skill, like making a sample, that is not co-inventing. Likewise, co-inventing is not assembling the invention or testing it. People whose contributions are solely obvious elements of the invention are not co-inventors, nor are people who are consulted before or after about the invention but are not part of the actual conception of the idea. Someone who thinks of the problem but doesn't contribute to the idea of how to solve the problem is not a co-inventor, and neither is a person who suggests an improvement but doesn't work to fit the improvement into the invention.

The reason it is important to include every person who is a co-inventor on the patent application is that leaving someone who should be listed off the patent can be grounds for invalidating the patent. And once invalidated, it will never be able to have patent protection again.

Some people have the misconception that you can take your idea, document it in some way, seal it in an envelope, and mail it to yourself, and that would serve to prove the idea was yours and the timeframe of that idea, and that would protect you if someone else knocked off your idea and tried to patent it. The strategy may or may not have worked many years ago, but it is guaranteed to not work today. Patent protection is given to the first to file, not the first to invent, so if you created an invention and didn't get it patented but someone else did, you're out of luck.

ii.   Trade Names, Trademarks, and Service Marks

Trademarks are words, symbols, or combinations of words and symbols that identifies one business' goods from another. Service marks are trademarks for service businesses, although the term trademark has come to be used for both goods based businesses and service based businesses. A trade name is a name used to identify a specific business, and is a type of trademark.

From this point forward, I'm only going to refer to trademarks but the information in the remainder of this section will apply equally to service marks.

Trademark protection is given automatically to the first person who starts using a word or symbol in business in their locale, usually defined by county. This protection is under what we call common law, and these common law rights prevent other people from using the same or similar words and symbols in the same or similar types of businesses in those counties.

Although you do not have to identify the words and symbols as being protected by trademark for them to be protected under the common law, it is a good idea if you do. The way to identify the trademark under common law is to put the TM (or SM in the case of a service mark) next to the words or symbols. When you have identified your trademark this way, it puts people on notice that you intend to exercise your trademark rights and because of that, damages for infringement are increased from what they would be if you had not used the trademark identifier. You do not have to make any registration to any government or agency before using the TM (or SM) symbol. Your words and symbols, however, do have to qualify for protection for the trademark to be enforceable. (More about that shortly)

You can register your trademark with the State of Minnesota for even more protection. When your trademark is registered with the state, your trademark infringement case is governed by statute (the laws created by the legislature) in addition to the common law (the laws created by the courts). Under the statute, you can get triple damages for violation of your Minnesota registered trademark, and your attorney's fees and costs, if the violation was "with knowledge" or "in bad faith."

Federal trademark protection is granted by the United States patent and trademark office (USPTO), and protects the words and symbols from being used by others nationwide for the classes of goods and services that the trademark has been registered under. Any businesses holding common law rights to those words and symbols before the trademark registration are allowed to continue using those words and symbols within the counties that they had established doing business in before the trademark registration, but they could not expand to new territories.

Federal trademark protection is intended for businesses that are going to sell their goods or services in more than one state. Technically, if you never intended to do business outside of your state then the Federal government doesn't need to extend trademark protection for areas where you will never do business.

When a business files for a registered trademark with the USPTO, the trademark registration relates back to when the application is received even though it may take a year or more to get the registration approved. Until the USPTO approves the trademark, you may not use the® symbol but you may use the common law TM symbol.

To qualify for trademark protection, the word or symbol has to have some level of distinction in relation to the product or service. A completely generic description has no distinctiveness and can be given no protection. An example of this would be aspirin pain reliever. From there, there is a spectrum of distinctiveness that provides ever increasing protection. Just above "no distinctiveness" is "not inherently distinctive." In this category, names would be descriptive, or geographic, or may contain a surname, and these names are considered weak and given little protection until they are so well known that they acquire distinctiveness by their reputation. In this category, notice of the intent to use the words or symbols as a trademark is very important. An example of this would be McDonald's restaurants.

The next three categories are all "inherently distinctive," but to varying degrees. The first is suggestive, and in this category the name has some connotation with the product or service but is not descriptive of that product or service. This category has strong and broad protection, with immediate protection available upon first use of the trademark. An example of this would be Coppertone suntan lotion. The next category is arbitrary, meaning that the word or symbol is something known but not before used or associated with that good or service. This category has even stronger and broader protection. An example of this would be Apple computers. The final and strongest category is coined or fanciful, meaning it is a made-up word or symbol that did not exist before the business started using it. An example of this is Clorox bleach.

Trademark protection can be kept indefinitely provided the trademark is being properly maintained. Once registered, the trademark must be renewed on time to have continued protection other than common law protection. To have continued common law protection, the trademark must be continued to be used in business.

For trademark infringement, the main test is whether or not the word or symbol is likely to cause confusion, or to cause mistake, or to deceive. For instance, using the word Nike on a pair of shoes would be an infringement of Nike's trademark, but using the word Nike for a flower shop would not be because the public does not associate flowers with the clothing and footwear company named Nike.

iii. Copyright essentials

Copyrights protect "original works of authorship" that are "fixed in a tangible medium of expression," meaning that they are observable. They include literary works, dramatic works like plays and movies, music, visual arts, architecture, and software code. It does not protect ideas, systems, or methods of doing things (which are instead protected by patents).

Copyright law automatically grants protection to the creators of copyrightable works, except for works made under a "work for hire" agreement, whether or not those works are ever registered in the U.S. copyright office. Copyright protection gives the copyright holder the exclusive right to reproduce the work, distribute copies of the work, perform and display the work publicly, and make derivative works based on the original work.

A "work for hire" arrangement is one where the creator is hired to create some intellectual property with the agreement that the intellectual property rights will belong to the person contracting to have the work made, and not the creator.

You should identify your copyrightable works with the © symbol (or using the word copyright) and the year of first publication. If those works change over time, like on a web site, put the date range from the year of first publication to the current year. While copyrightable works are automatically protected, using the copyright symbol puts people on notice that the work is intended to be protected, and so you can get more damages in an infringement lawsuit than you would if you did not use the copyright symbol.

You do not need to register with the United States copyright office to be protected, but there are some benefits if you do, like being able to bring a copyright infringement lawsuit in federal court (as opposed to state court) and statutory damages and attorney's fees being available in federal court if the copyright was registered within three months of the work's publication.

There are limitations on copyright protection. For instance, a work that is a "useful article" is something that is designed to serve a utilitarian purpose, like an article of clothing, or a car, or piece of furniture. A useful article can have aspects that are not copyrightable and aspects that are copyrightable. Copyright never protects the utilitarian or mechanical aspects of the useful article, but the pictorial, graphic, or sculptural designs that can be identified separately from, or exist independently of, the utilitarian aspects of the article are copyrightable. For instance, a t-shirt design would not be copyrightable but the graphic printed on it would be.

Another limitation on copyright protection is the "fair use" doctrine. This doctrine allows brief excerpts to be used for purposes of criticism, news reporting, teaching, and research provided that the material is quoted verbatim. Another important doctrine is the "first sale" doctrine which allows a person who buys copyrighted material the right to sell, display, or dispose of that copy of the work. Those rights end when the individual disposes of that copy of the work.

Copyrights last for the life of the author plus an additional 70 years unless the work is created under a "work for hire" agreement, in which case the copyright lasts for the lessor of 95 years from the date of first publication or 120 years from the date of creation.

Copyright infringement can bring both criminal charges as well as civil damages. Ignorance is no excuse for infringement, and the copyright holder can bring a suit whenever an infringement occurs. Many types of copyright infringement carry hefty statutory penalties along with an award of attorneys' fees and costs, so violations can be very expensive.

iv.   Shhhh! (Trade Secrets)

A trade secret is proprietary information that a company keeps secret because it gets economic value from the secret, and if someone else also had that secret disclosed to them or they could easily figure it out, then that other person could also get the economic value from it. The information could be a recipe, formula, program, device, method, technique, process, or pattern. For a trade secret to keep its status as such, and continued intellectually property protection, the business has to take "reasonable efforts" to protect it, which generally means that employees are required to sign confidentiality agreements, secret documents are kept in locked files, secret materials are distributed on a "need to know" basis, visitors are restricted to visiting areas with non-secret processes, and sensitive processes are handled apart from the central facility.

The classic example of a trade secret is the Coca-Cola formula (no pun intended). The company has maintained some mystery around their formula for the past 100+ years. In their case, they've managed to make the secrecy of their formula something of a marketing tool.

Customer lists are not likely to be protected in and of itself, unless there is a compelling reason to do so, but a particular process that a company uses to sell to its customers along with a customer list could be a trade secret if the company designates it as such and takes reasonable efforts to protect that information.

If someone takes a trade secret and discloses it, the company can as the court to prevent the person or company that the trade secret was disclosed to from using the information (called injunctive relief) and can order that money damages be paid to the trade secret holder. If the trade secret was actively stolen, the trade secret holder could get extra damages up to twice the amount of money of the initial damages.

b. Protecting and enforcing your intellectual property rights

What you have intellectual property rights, whether that is a patent, trademark, copyright, or trade secret, the responsibility of protecting and enforcing your intellectual property rights lies solely with you. It is your responsibility to be diligent in searching out possible infringers from time to time.

If the infringer becomes known to you and you do nothing, your allowing them to continue using your intellectual property rights will be considered to be consensual, and if you tried to sue them for infringement later down the road your lawsuit could be dismissed under doctrine called latches. Under the doctrine of latches, you have to bring the case shortly after you learn of the damage to you. If you knowingly let someone continue, you could not have been that damaged and the court will not waste its resources on helping you.

c. Defending yourself if you've violated the rights of others

The way it will likely happen is that you'll get a letter in the mail notifying you that you're using someone's intellectual property and that they demand that you stop. The most likely source of a violation would be using someone else's copyrighted material or having a trade name or trademark too similar to that of a competitor.

If the demand letter is regarding a copyright infringement, the thing to do is to see where you're using the material, and see if you have a license to use it. Also see if the use is permissible under the "fair use" doctrine. If you have a license or your use of the material falls under the fair use doctrine, then make a copy of the license and evidence of your payment or document why your use is allowable under the fair use doctrine, and send copies of those materials with the letter to the attorney who sent you a demand letter.

If it turns out that you do not have a license to use the material and its use is not subject to the fair use doctrine, then you could be liable for the infringement. Damages under statutory law can be very high and an unintentional or accidental use of someone else's copyrighted material qualifies for those damages. They don't have to show that your violation was willful, and you do not have accident or mistake as a defense.

The best thing to do is to stop using the material, and negotiate some copyright fee with the copyright holder in exchange for dropping the copyright infringement case. You may end up paying more than you think you should for whatever it was that was the source of the problem, but whatever you pay will be significantly less than lawsuit defense and statutory damages.

In the case of a trademark infringement claim, you'll want to look at your trademark and their trademark and see if there's enough similarity that there could be some likelihood of confusion. You'll want to research the other company to see if they in the same or similar industry as you. Lastly, you'll want to research when they started using that mark, if they registered it, and if they did not register it, wet areas they used it in and when. If you started using the mark before them in your area, then your rights to use it are senior to theirs. If your marks are similar but you are in completely different industries, with a low likelihood of confusion between you and the other mark holder, then you may have a strong defense. Depending on what you find in the research, you may want to try to hold onto your mark or you may be willing to make a change. Even if you're in the right, it may cost you something to defend your right to your mark. You'll have to weigh the costs of defense against the cost of changing your mark. Before you do anything, though, you should get the opinion of a lawyer who's experienced in trademark disputes.

For any intellectual property violation demand letter that you get, it would be well worth the money to have a consultation with an intellectual property rights attorney to know the potential damages, your potential defenses, and to create an effective strategy for handling the matter.

Chapter 6: Welcome to the jungle (the commercial real estate world is not always a friendly place)

In the world of residential real estate there are many legal protections put in place for buyers and tenants, and in many regards the laws are written to give tenants a good amount of grace, often at the landlord's expense. Not so in the commercial real estate world. In the commercial real estate world, business owners are presumed to be savvy individuals who are capable of negotiating the best terms possible for themselves. This means that commercial leases are most often written to favor the landlord and owner over the tenant in ways that would be extreme, unconscionable, and illegal in the residential real estate world. Welcome to the jungle, indeed.

a. A few specific things to watch out for

i. What kind of lease do you have?

Commercial real estate leases come in three basic varieties and the structure of your lease and the rights you have will vary widely depending on what type of lease you are being offered.

1. Gross

If you've been offered a gross lease, consider yourself lucky. Of the three types of leases, a gross lease has the most potential of favoring the tenant and certainly has the effect of limiting your liability in comparison to the other lease types.

A gross lease is one where your rent payment includes all services and utilities. In other words, you pay a fixed amount regardless of the building maintenance costs and utilities costs to the owner.

2. Net

A net lease is one where the tenant pays a base rent amount, plus their share of the building's "usual costs", things like property management fees, maintenance, repairs, utilities, insurance, and taxes. A "double net" lease will include rent plus tax and insurance, and a "triple net" lease will include rent plus maintenance, taxes, and insurance. A net lease generally favors the landlord.

3. Percentage

A percentage lease is one where there is a base rent plus a certain percentage of sales. This type of lease is commonly found in retail strip malls, shopping malls, and other locations for retail stores and restaurants. With a percentage lease, you will likely be required to have your business open to the public for certain days and hours, and you will be in breach of the lease if you "go dark" or don't open your doors when you are supposed to.

ii. What maintenance and repairs might you be responsible for?

1. Common Area Maintenance (CAM)

Common Area Maintenance (CAM) will definitely be a part of a triple net lease, but may also be a part of a percentage lease. CAM expenses may include electricity, water and sewer, janitorial, repairs, snow removal, window washing, and property management. It is usually calculated by your square footage ÷ the total square footage of the building x the costs to run the building. You may be paying an estimated CAM on a monthly basis and then be sent a bill (or credit) at the end of the year based on actual expenses. One year, the CAM adjustment on my triple net lease for my office space had me responsible for paying an additional $14,000 in January.

2. HVAC *equipment*

Repair and maintenance of HVAC equipment, and sometimes even replacement, will likely be a part of your net lease and percentage lease if that equipment services your space exclusively. If it services the spaces for multiple tenants or the building as a whole, it will be part of the CAM expenses.

Before you sign a lease with an HVAC equipment obligation, especially with a replacement obligation, you should have a commercial HVAC professional inspect the equipment and report to you its age, condition, and likelihood of failure. If the equipment is old and unlikely to outlive the term of your lease, you may want to either negotiate that term to have some cap or limit on your liability, or you may want to keep looking for space. In our negotiations on behalf of clients, we've had some landlords accept a reasonable cap and we've had others refuse to change the lease.

3. *Windows*

Tenant's liability for damage to glass is common in net leases and percentage leases, and in a commercial space there can be a lot of glass. It is important that your commercial insurance policy has sufficient coverage for the amount of window square footage you are responsible for, and having a specific glass policy rider is a good idea.

4. *Plumbing*

In a net lease or percentage lease, if certain plumbing services your space exclusively, like in a hair salon or a dog grooming business, or where your space has its own dedicated bathrooms or kitchen, you will likely be responsible for the maintenance and repair of the plumbing system, including plumbing fixtures and hot water heaters. If it is not specifically called out in your lease, then it will be a part of CAM.

5. *Signage*

Especially in percentage leases, but also possible in net leases, the landlord may have signage requirements that you are responsible for complying with at your own costs. For instance, in a strip mall you may be responsible for procuring the sign for your business that will be a part of the mall's entrance sign by the road and the sign outside your door, to the specifications and approval of the landlord, using their vendor.

If you are allowed to select your own vendor, be sure that you select one that is approved for your city. If you buy your signage from someone who is not approved, you may end up paying again for the exact same signage but from an approved vendor. You will be responsible for the costs of installation when you move in and the removal when you move out.

iii.   Improvements

All leasehold improvements belong to the landlord in every type of lease. How it works is that you are leasing the space in a certain condition, and that space can be changed to fit your needs either at your expense (with their approval of your plans, of course) or by them with a build-out allowance (which you will ultimately pay for with an increased rent rate for the life of your lease). Anything that is "attached" to the property becomes an improvement that belongs to the landlord. In addition to the obvious things like walls and doors, this includes light fixtures, network cabling, plumbing additions, and cabinetry. It can include a custom built-in reception desk. Leasehold improvements can be very expensive and its money that you are never going to get back.

iv.   The personal guarantee

Every commercial lease I've seen, and I've seen many, requires a personal guarantee of the business owner. The obligation on the commercial lease is often one of the costliest expenses for a business, and when you translate that obligation into personal terms, it can be staggering and quite frightening. A modest lease at $5,000 per month for a modest term of 3 years is a personal obligation of $180,000 for the business owner if things go sideways. (And that's with a modest lease)

You're not going to get out of giving a personal guarantee on your commercial lease, so you'll need to get comfortable with some economic risk. That said, there's a couple of things that we try to negotiate in that will help to defray the impact to you. The first is a right to sublet with their consent *which will not be unreasonably withheld*. With those magic words included, they can reject someone because their credit or financials have them not qualify for the lease, but not because they want to be punitive, or because they prefer blondes, or just because. With that provision, you may have to hustle to get a replacement tenant, but for every month that tenant pays, your personal liability goes down.

The other provision is explicitly stating that the landlord has *a duty to mitigate its losses*, which means that the landlord has the obligation to try to lease to someone else and curtail their damages (and the amount you are on the hook for). This is the default provision in residential leases (and most contracts, really, under general contract principles) but is usually the opposite in most commercial leases. Most commercial leases explicitly state that the landlord has no duty to mitigate, and that leaves you on the hook and at the mercy of the landlord to take action.

Let's look at the worst-case scenario that could happen. You enter into a costly commercial lease for a seven-year term, and in year two you realize that you can't make this business work and you want out. You have 60 months of obligation that will hit you personally if you terminate the lease early. This is one of the situations where a personal bankruptcy may be an option. If you have the choice between sacrificing five years of your life to fulfill on the obligation or getting the thing discharged, take the bankruptcy and move on with your life. Yes, you would have a smudge on your credit for a time. Is your life worth less to you than your credit score? I hope not. I don't often advocate for bankruptcy, but it is a tool that is available to you and knowing that can help you be ready to take the risk if you want, or need, to enter into a commercial lease.

v.   Breach and remedies

Breach means not fulfilling on the obligations of the contract, and can include many more things than terminating the lease early or failing to make payments. It can mean a failure to maintain something that was supposed to be maintained, it could be being so disruptive that the neighbors can't effectively use their space, it could be using the space for something other than the permitted use. The big ones, of course, are not paying rent (for you) and not maintaining the property (for the landlord), so we're going to frame our discussion around those things.

1.   *If you breach the lease agreement*

In every commercial lease I've seen, and I've seen many, the remedies available to a landlord if a tenant breaches is long and comprehensive. A common and insidious remedy is eviction without termination (which means you are booted out of the space, but that the obligation under the contract still stands, so the landlord will not and cannot get a replacement tenant and the space will sit vacant while you pay for space you don't get to use). There are instances when the lease agreement allows a UCC security interest in the business' inventory and other assets, or even your own personal assets, to be filed.

The landlord can bring a lawsuit for money damages and accelerate the whole amount due under the contract, or there may be a specific amount of liquidated damages called for in the contract (a damage amount that is set forth in advance because it would be difficult if not impossible to ascertain the actual amount and the liquidated damages amount is a reasonable approximation of the probable loss). And, of course, you'll lose your security deposit.

2. If your landlord breaches the lease agreement

Commercial lease agreements are written to give the landlord all the benefits it can get with as few obligations as it can get away with. In most commercial leases, the tenant has no right to offset (reduce the amount of rent in exchange for taking care of an obligation that the landlord should have but did not) unless they have negotiated it into the lease (usually with a notice requirement, time frame for the landlord to act, and a cap on the amount that the tenant is allowed to offset).

In retail space leases, there are sometimes exclusivity clauses that are part of the lease, meaning that the landlord cannot let a direct competitor to you into the mall. In those instances, if the landlord allows a competing business to lease in violation of the exclusivity clause, you would have the right to go to the court and ask the court to prevent the landlord from leasing to the competitor (called injunctive relief). Depending on what terms were negotiated, you may have a right to lost profits or liquidated damages, but only if you negotiated to have those terms included.

vi. Risk of being moved

When you are a smaller tenant, the lease will often allow the landlord to move you to another similar space in order to consolidate spaces to make room for a larger tenant. If your business relies on people coming in through a heavily trafficked corridor, and you are moved to a remote corner that no one but the mall joggers knows exists, your business could be tanked even though technically the space was comparable in terms of size and layout.

If you are a smaller tenant and your lease gives the landlord the right to move you, it is important to negotiate the contract to identify the specific things that will make the space comparable to you, like access to parking, traffic volume on that corridor, or proximity to attractions like the movie theatre. Whatever are the key points that had you select the location you are considering, you need to get those articulated into the lease agreement.

b. A few specific things to ask for, if applicable

i. Rent concessions

Commercial real estate investors look at something called the capitalization rate, or cap rate for short, which is the return on the investment that the property is expected to bring in based on the rental income. The figures that go into the cap rate are (base rents – operating expenses) ÷ current market value of the property.

Aggressive commercial real estate investors also often hold a property for a five-year period and then flip it. Not always, but often. Commercial real estate changes hands much more often than you might think.

Why does this make a difference to you? Because when the real estate investor is getting ready to flip the building, they want to show a nice, high cap rate, which means that the price per square foot is going to be a bit elevated. Cap rate calculations come from base rent, so they aren't going to want to give you a deal on the rent amount on paper, but they can give you a deal on the total amount you actually pay with rent concessions. For instance, your base rent may be $5,000 per month, but you get two months of rent concessions to sign the lease, and now you pay $50,000 instead of $60,000. They show $5,000 for the cap rate calculation but you, in effect, are only paying $4,166.66.

If they won't budge on the price, it's always a good idea to ask about concessions.

ii. Buildout allowance

If the space you are considering is not already built out in a way that serves your purposes, it will need to be altered. Sometimes the landlord takes on doing the build out, and sometimes that tenant takes responsibility. When the landlord does the build out, often they will give a build out allowance, of so much per square foot, depending on what they are willing to offer and what is adequate to make your space workable. Then you work with their architect and crew, pick out your colors and finishes, and they handle the project management and construction.

Keep in mind that a commercial build out is no cheap endeavor. I once dropped over $5,000 just taking down a wall between two offices. A whole build out can easily cost in the hundreds of thousands of dollars, depending on the size and scope of the project. The landlord is in essence extending credit to you for the build out costs and you're in essence going to pay it back over time in the form of a premium rent payment. If you can't afford to foot the construction costs upfront, this is a really good option if you get the opportunity offered to you.

    iii.   Special construction

Certain types of businesses have particular needs in how its space is constructed. In my office, we have sound attenuation batt between the offices and conference rooms so private conversations are private, and that's important in a law office. The standard for privacy is even more rigorous in doctor's offices and therapist's offices.

Other types of businesses need special construction considerations, like how a florist shop has to have special electrical outlets run to accommodate the refrigerated flower cases. Or how a beauty shop has to have five sinks (and the drain plumbing) in a row. If those special things get left out, the business just won't function.

Whatever your particular business' needs as far as special construction, it is imperative that 1) the purpose of your business is explicitly stated in the lease agreement and 2) that the special construction needs are explicitly stated in the contract as something the landlord is responsible for delivering.

iv. Option to renew

Whenever possible, I always like to have the option, but not the obligation, to renew. If you don't negotiate an option to renew into the lease, then at the end of the term the landlord could choose not to renew with you, regardless of whether or not you always paid your rent on time and were a good tenant. An option to renew usually has some time frame before the end of the lease term in which to notify the landlord of your intent to exercise the option. The option gives you the right to renew, but the rental term will often be renegotiated. If you can't negotiate a rental rate that works for you, you don't have the obligation to renew.

If you have invested into leasehold improvements, paid for marketing efforts for the public to know where to find you, and built a good reputation in your locale, why would you risk losing all that at the whim of a landlord? Get an option to renew.

v. First right of refusal on neighboring space

If you have plans, even far off dreams, to expand your business at some point, then negotiate a first right of refusal on the neighboring space to yours (provided there is neighboring space, of course). It would work like this: your neighbor would move out and the landlord would let you know that their space was opening up.

At that time, you could negotiate and take the space if you wanted. If you weren't quite ready to do that though, you don't actually exercise the first right of refusal until the landlord has someone who is interested in taking the space and some specific terms are nailed down.

You see, you can't refuse something until it is offered to you, and in a first right of refusal there has to be some third party that has made or accepted an offer that defines those terms. Once that happens, the landlord brings you the offer and you have the first right to take the deal under those terms, or refuse it and the other person will take the space. Generally, you need to be ready to decide quickly. First rights of first refusal are open for a matter of days, not weeks or months.

vi. Caps on expenses

CAM charges can get really out of hand, and you have no control over them. If you can get the landlord to entertain it, then negotiate a cap on CAM charges, after which you will not be responsible for that year's expenses. And while you're at it, negotiate that CAM expenses cannot increase more than a certain percentage from one year to the next, somewhere above 3% to keep pace with inflation but something less than 5% to keep expenses in check.

vii. Percentage after initial sales

If you have a percentage lease, negotiate the amount of sales after which the percentage will apply. For instance, the percentage does not apply to the first $5,000 in sales, or whatever number makes sense in your business. If the percentage applies to the first dollar on, and you don't make enough sales (which can happen when you're new), then you'll be even more in the hole at the end of the month.

c. When do you need professional help?

I've done lease reviews and analysis for leases that were literally over 50 pages of small print, written in dense legalese. If you're given anything close to that nature, seek professional help. Even if you think you understand the lease, you may want to seek professional help. Commercial leases are not written with your well-being in mind. You need to know what you're getting yourself into.

d. When do you take the deal?

More than once I've had a client who took the deal, despite the landlord refusing to negotiate reasonable provisions, despite the likelihood of having to replace a thirty-year-old furnace within the last year of the contract, and despite having no renewal options after making a significant financial investment. Why? Because something about the location was perfect for what they were up to. You take the deal when the space is right and you can live with the terms, no matter how unsavory they may be, and then you just make it work. Set aside cash for the furnace. Be charming to the person who holds your renewal fate in their hands. Things like that.

Chapter 7: Creating and keeping solid agreements (the basics of making and enforcing contracts)

At its core, business is all about relationships. You may think you sell a good or service, but if you don't have relationships with your customers you're not selling anything, and you'll have no business. If you don't have relationships with your vendors and suppliers, you won't have what you need to serve your customers, and you'll have no business. If you don't have relationships with the people who work for you, nothing will get done, and you'll have no business.

Contracts are also all about relationships. If you want your business to succeed, you should get very good at relationships and become a big fan of contracts. Contracts set forth the expectations of the relationship and set rules around unmet expectations.

a. What does it take to make an enforceable agreement?

In order to have an enforceable agreement, 1) someone has to make an offer, 2) someone else has to accept that offer, 3) the people involved have to have capacity (and authority) to enter into the agreement, 4) they have to be mutually obligated, 5) there has to be some bargained-for exchange (called consideration), and 6) the contract has to be for some lawful purpose.

The first two elements are pretty easy to understand. The third element is capacity in an individual sense (is the person over the age of 18, not impaired by drugs or medical conditions) and authority in a business context (what is their role in the company, has the board granted them agency authority to bind the company).

The fourth element, mutual obligation, means that both sides are obligated to perform something under the contract. It may be to pay something, it may be to do something, or it may be to refrain from doing something. If only one party is obligated and the other party can choose to do or not do, then it's not a valid contract. Sometimes complicated gifts look like contracts, but when the recipient will get the benefit of the gift whether they do something or not, it's not a contract, it's a gift.

The fifth element, consideration, is also known as the "quid pro quo" of the agreement. This is the part where someone says, "I'll give you cash in exchange for your car." Sometimes its hard to see what the bargained for exchange may be in a contract, like when it appears that you would have entered into the agreement whether or not a certain provision was in the contract. When that happens, for the contract to be enforceable, the consideration has to be spelled out as such. An example would be, "The grant of this Option is the consideration and without the grant of the Option, party A would not have entered into this agreement."

The last element is that the contract has to be for some lawful purpose. You can't have a contract to break the law and have it be enforceable, and that's probably why drug dealers and pimps don't have their "crew" execute noncompete agreements.

b.   He said/She said (the pitfalls of oral agreements)

With some notable exceptions covered in the next section, an oral agreement is fully enforceable provided that it meets all the elements of a contract from the previous section. That said, oral agreements can be difficult. First of all, human memory is not perfect. Second of all, people have different understandings even if they're hearing the same words. Anyone who is married can attest to that.

The problem with oral agreements is that it is hard to know if everyone really is on the same page as far as who is doing what, and when, and in exchange for what. By the time some conflict arises, people have already been performing on the contract doing the part that they thought was theirs to do. At that point, it's difficult to get people to regroup and start from the beginning to get any misunderstandings ironed out. Mostly people just assume the other side is breaking the agreement because they're not doing what was expected.

If you have an oral agreement and it appears to be going sideways, you often can bring it to court but you might not want to. Here's why: in a written contract case, there's lots of time spent on who did what, and why, and what they should've done instead, and so on, but they spend very little time arguing over what the contract says because you can just read it; it's no mystery.

In an oral contract case, you have all that same time spent on who did what, and why, and so forth that you have in the other with the addition of a whole lot of time spent hashing out what everybody's understanding of the contract was. The case is going to take longer and cost more, and the outcome is going to be even more uncertain than in a case with a written contract.

If you have and an oral agreement and it appears to be going sideways, the better course is to stop and get clear about your understanding and the other side's understanding about the contract, and try to get things back on track.

c.   Satisfying the Statute of Frauds

There are certain contracts that must be in writing to be enforceable, and the list of those contracts are found in the law under the "Statute of Frauds." The list of contracts that must be in writing are 1) contracts for the sale of goods for the price of $500 or more, 2) contracts which cannot be performed within one year, 3) contracts for the transfer of an interest in land, and 4) contracts that obligate a party to be a surety (i.e., guarantor).

d. Getting it in writing (even informally)

Not every agreement has to be reduced to a formal contract, and often in business getting the agreement terms documented in an informal process, like in an email chain, is sufficient.

A written agreement that lays out the obligations for each party involved is legally binding and does not necessarily require a lawyer's input. However, to be effective (as opposed to enforceable) it must be a clear, detailed, comprehensive and unambiguous record of the agreed upon terms to head off possible disagreements.

You can document a basic business agreement without too much hassle. Simply send the proposed terms of the contract to the other parties and request confirmation that all the terms are written up correctly. If you have agreement on all the terms, the written memorialization of it will help you navigate any issues that may come up and even provide evidence of the parties' obligations if you do end up in court.

If it turns out that your understanding of the terms is different than their understanding of the terms, it's better to get that ironed out before you start doing business, and you may not have discovered that you didn't have a common understanding if you hadn't sent the confirmation of the terms.

What points are most essential? Here are four of the fundamentals:

- Scope - Remember that you are memorializing an agreement – so be like a journalist getting the whole picture. You need to detail Who, What, Where, and Why. Don't forget to include the measurable result that indicates the obligation has been met, or if a measurable result isn't possible in that circumstance, indicate who evaluates that a task has been satisfactorily completed – otherwise you could find that one person thinks they performed the contract and the other thinks otherwise.

- Time - Lay out a schedule. Specify the duration of the agreement and any important deadlines. Milestones are best established beforehand so that all parties know what to expect. Payment, too, is definitively best scheduled.

- Payment - Again, precision is key. The entirety of the payment process ought to be written out–who will pay whom, what form will that payment take, and when will it occur? Don't forget to put in place clear consequences for late payment.

- Disputes - No matter how much you scrutinize each line of a contract, disputes can still arise. That's why it is so vital to determine how conflicts will be handled before one breaks out. Often, businesses opt to submit matters to mediation or arbitration before proceeding to court – while it's not always less expensive (although it can be), mediation and arbitration is not a matter of public record (no bad press) and the potential for resolving the dispute in a positive way that provides for the possibility of continuing a good working relationship is much higher than when going through the court process.

Mediation and arbitration only happen by agreement, so you need to have it in your contract if you want to stay out of court. Don't forget to specify which state's law will govern the dispute, as well as who is responsible for legal fees.

While the above is a solid framework for a basic business agreement, you should never put yourself in the position of being uncertain about a contract you've put together–a contract can quickly expand in complexity and threaten to trip you up with a seemingly minor detail. That's when you need to call in an experienced business lawyer to read through the fine print and ensure you get the maximum protection possible.

It can even be a good idea to create a template for certain types of agreements you use frequently–you can create the template and have a lawyer review once, and then you'll have it on hand to use over and over whenever you need it.

Whether the agreement is with clients, vendors, partners, or anyone else, never neglect to get a written document that will have your back. Not only does it protect your business, it will demonstrate to the other party that you take the relationship seriously. Likewise, if the other party proposes forgoing a written contract, you should look long and hard at why that might be.

e. The usual boilerplate (which is not as standard as you might think and is critical to get right)

People often come into my office and asked me to give them the "usual contract" for whatever their situation is, and I am always surprised by that for two reasons. First, why come to a lawyer like me who focuses on creating carefully tailored, ironclad agreements only to ask for something so generic you could drive a Mack truck through the holes in its protection? Second, the idea of the "usual contract" is a bit of a myth. While it's true that you can find some templated version of many contracts on the Internet, that doesn't mean that there's one master version that we're all working from.

I think people have this idea of one master agreement that we have in our back pocket because there are certain terms that often show up over and over again in almost every contract. We call those terms "boilerplate" and some people think they are less important than the other terms of the contract. I disagree. Mostly the things that people explicitly talk about when negotiating a contract are those things from the previous section, scope, time, payment, and dispute resolution. People are rarely talking about the boilerplate provisions, which mostly have to do with the rules around rights and obligations if there's a conflict.

If no one looks at the boilerplate until there's a conflict, then they're likely going to be surprised by the rules and rights that are listed there. These provisions can be tailored favorably towards one party or the other, or they can be rather balanced and neutral. When I create a contract, I look at my client's purpose and I tailor those boilerplate provisions to meet that purpose. It is critical to get those technical aspects of the contract right because what is in those sections often determines who wins and who loses.

f.   Enforcing the agreement if you have to

The methods of enforcing the agreement available to you depends on what the contract says about that, and if the contract is silent on the point then you have the full scope of legal remedies available to you.

Some contracts specify that the parties go to mediation (facilitated settlement talks) or arbitration (private judge process) before seeking court intervention. If that is the case, then that is the procedure you follow. Even if the contract doesn't specify that the parties go to mediation or arbitration first, it is often useful to see if they are open to doing that. For most businesses, there's value in staying out of the public court system and resolving differences privately. Also, mediation or arbitration can be done more quickly than litigation, even if it's not always cheaper.

Depending on the circumstances and the value of the contract, a lawsuit may or may not be a good idea. Under contract law, you can only get the amount of damages required "to make you whole" and not punitive damages (extra damages awarded to punish the defendant), although sometimes clients are so angry about the breach of contract that they think punitive damages are in order. If the amount of damages is low and the time and hassle it will take to prove your case is high, a lawsuit is likely not going to be your best option. On the other hand, if the value of the contract is high and you have almost all the evidence you need from the outset, a lawsuit may be one of your good options. If you cannot get the other party to cooperate in the process, you may have to bring a lawsuit whether or not your case is such that a lawsuit is your best option.

I find that a certain amount of the time we can get the matter resolved with some communication and negotiation. When we make the attempt and either our communications are rebuffed or negotiations break down, that's when we have to turn to our next strategy, whether that is mediation, arbitration, or full-on litigation.

g. Breaching the agreement if you need to

I grew up being taught that going back on your word was one of the worst things a person could ever do. Imagine my surprise when I was taught in law school about the concept of the beneficial breach. It turns out that you always have the right to breach a contract, to go back on your word; you'll just have to deal with the consequences of that breach. The concept of a beneficial breach is that if the consequences to you of breaching the contract are less than the cost to you of fulfilling on the contract, then it is to your benefit to breach and you should do it.

Personally, I would take more than just economic factors into consideration before I would recommend a breach. I would consider the relationship with the other party and how the breach may impact that, the value of that relationship now and into the future, and the impact that the breach may have on other relationships with third parties who aren't a part of the agreement, but may be impacted by it. I'd take a holistic view before pulling the trigger, but know that it is an option that is available to you.

Chapter 8: Hiring employees

One of the most exciting milestones in a business' growth is when it needs to add staff. How you do that is one of the most important decisions that you'll ever make in your business. And by that, I don't mean the skill sets or personal attributes of your potential staff member (although those are important too), what I mean is figuring out whether or not your new hire is an independent contractor or an employee, and the process that you go through to hire them.

The next four chapters are all interrelated and have a lot of technical stuff in them, but it is actually not all that comprehensive in the world of employment regulations and issues. I've hit the high-points, and left plenty of important things out entirely. To do a really good job, these topics would need to be a different book in its entirety.

Plus, this is one area of law where the rules are constantly changing and even if I could have made a comprehensive primer, it very well may have been out of date before the printing presses cooled off. There are some very good resources available on the web, though, that have a much broader and deeper scope than this chapter and are likely to be kept up to date, and I encourage you to check them out when it comes time for you to hire and fire.

An Employer's Guide to Employment Law Issues in Minnesota (put out by the Minnesota Department of Employment and Economic Development): https://mn.gov/deed/assets/an-employers-guide-to-employment-law-issues-in-minnesota-14th-ed-2018_tcm1045-133700.pdf

Employment Practices (website from Minnesota Department of Labor and Industry):
https://www.dli.mn.gov/business/employment-practices

A Legal Guide to the Use of Social Media in the Workplace (put out by the Minnesota Department of Employment and Economic

Development): https://mn.gov/deed/assets/legal-guide-social-media-workplace_tcm1045-133709.pdf

a. When is a staff member an employee?

While you may think of anyone who works for you as an "employee," in reality an employee is a specific employment status that has certain rights, and you have certain rights in their work product. If someone isn't an employee, they don't have those same rights as an employee, but you also don't have the same rights in their work product unless you create a specific agreement stating that you do. In your workplace culture, everyone may be treated the same as "staff members," but nonetheless it is important to distinguish who is in what category and make sure you have the right legal documentation in place for each one.

i. Who isn't your employee?

1. *Independent contractors*

An independent contractor is a person or business that provides services (and conceivably goods) to a business on a contractual basis. They have no rights outside of those specified in the contract.

2. *Trainees and interns*

Trainees and interns are not employees if this Department of Labor test is satisfied in all aspects:

- The training is similar to what would be given in a vocational school or academic educational instruction.
- The training is for the benefit of the trainees or students.
- The trainees or students do not displace regular employees, but work under their close observation.

- The employer that provides the training derives no immediate advantage from the activities of the trainees or students, and on occasion the employer's operations may actually be impeded.
- The trainees or students are not necessarily entitled to a job at the conclusion of the training period.
- The employer and the trainees or students understand that the trainees or students are not entitled to wages for the time spent in training.

If any of these criteria are not satisfied, then the trainee or intern is, in fact, an employee and must be paid and treated as such.

3. *Volunteers*

People who volunteer or donate their services for public service, religious, or humanitarian purposes without compensation are not considered employees of the religious, charitable or similar non-profit organizations that receive their service. *For-profit businesses may not have volunteers.*

4. *Somebody else's employees*

The employees of another person or business, like the employee of a vendor or an employee of an independent contractor, are not your employees even if they are working at your workplace and working closely with your employees at the direction of their employer.

ii. Everyone else = your employee

If the person does not fit in any of the allowed categories above (not a volunteer if you have a for-profit business), then they are, in fact, your employee. Employees can be full time or part time, temporary or permanent, and they can be recruited from a public job posting or they can be someone you know well, and the same rules and regulations will apply to all of them.

b.   The basics of hiring employees

Hiring employees is one of the most stressful things a business owner does, possibly only eclipsed by the stress of firing an employee. One source of hiring stress is the worry over whether or not you're doing it right since botched hiring processes can be a source of expensive litigation with declined applicants. Another source of hiring stress is being able to accurately assess the potential hire's qualifications without crossing the line, and this sometimes leaves business owners not getting the information they have a right to access either because of lack of knowledge or out of fear of being sued.

Many small business owners turn to a human resources consultant for help with the hiring (and even firing) process. This is a good idea when you are opening a job posting up to the public. Often, a business' first hires are friends or family members of the owner, and while that offers a whole different set of potential issues, there is generally less need for a human resources consultant in those instances.

As a business owner, you need to know the rules that apply to employees regardless of whether they are a stranger off the street or your brother-in-law.

i.   The Application

The laws related to employment have so many traps for the unwary that it is important to make sure that the information you are requesting is reasonably related to the job. Extra questions may accidentally reveal a person's status as a member of a protected class (see the protected classes in the next section).

Minnesota has a "Ban the Box" law which prohibits employers from asking about an applicant's criminal history until after an interview or until after a conditional offer of employment is made if there is no interview. You can, however, put a notice on the application that the job is conditioned upon passing a criminal background check.

You shouldn't assume that preprinted applications or forms you find on the internet will work for the job you are hiring for. They may be too broad for the job, and they may be from other states which do not have the same laws as Minnesota.

1. *Protected Classes*

There is a patchwork of federal and Minnesota laws that create the protected classes. These are the ones that you need to watch out for:

- Race
- Color
- Creed
- Religion
- National origin
- Age
- Sex (including sexual orientation and gender identity)
- Pregnancy
- Citizenship
- Marital Status
- Familial status
- Disability status
- Veteran status
- Genetic information
- Public Assistance Status
- Local Human Rights Commission Activity

2. *Using Disclaimers*

You may want to use disclaimers on your application and in your employee handbook to help keep you out of legal hot water. Disclaimers must be clear and conspicuous and a signed acknowledgement regarding the employee being given the handbook is helpful. Some good provisions to include in your disclaimers are:

- You retain the right to terminate the employment for any reason not prohibited by law and at any time.
- The employee retains the right to resign from employment at any time and for any reason.
- Any agreements to the contrary regarding employment must be in writing and signed by the owner (or an officer) of the company.
- The application, offer of employment letter, and employee handbook do not constitute an employment agreement and the employee handbook may be revised by employer at their sole discretion at any time.
- (If being issued for the first time) The employee handbook supersedes all previously issued policies.

ii. The interview (What you can (and can't) ask people)

When interviewing, you should only ask questions that relate to the job you are hiring for, otherwise your questions may reveal an applicant's status as a member of a protected class. If you learn of some information about an applicant's protected status in an interview, you may have to later show that you didn't use that information in the hiring process. That can be a tough thing to show.

When you interview applicants, do not make notes on the application itself. Instead, take notes on a separate notepad and discard those notes after an applicant has been hired.

Avoid making statements that indicate the applicant will have the job for a long time; those statements may reduce your right to let that person go later.

Some of the interview topics you should avoid:

- Anything to do with gender, race, creed, religion, national origin, or sexual orientation
- How old someone is, their birthdate, or what year they graduated from high school or college
- Their marital status, or what their spouse thinks of the job, what the spouse will think about the salary, or what their spouse does for work
- If they have children, or how many children they have, or their children's ages, or if they intend to have (more) children
- Who will care for their children while they are at work, or if they will quit the job if they become pregnant
- What languages are spoken in their home
- Military, National Guard or Reserve status, or date of military discharge
- Disabilities, physical conditions, or if they have a physical limitation that would impact the job
- If they ever received Worker's Compensation benefits
- How much they weigh, how tall they are, or if they smoke
- If they have ever been hospitalized, or treated for mental condition, or how many days they called in sick at a previous job
- If they take any medications, or if they have been treated for drug addiction or alcoholism
- If they have good credit, or if their wages have ever been garnished
- If they have ever been arrested

iii.   Using background checks

For some jobs, the law requires that applicants undergo a background check. Employers may also require a background check when the need is reasonably related to the job. Employers have a duty to not negligently hire and supervise employees, which means that you have a duty to make sure that the people you hire are appropriate and safe for the jobs they perform, or else you could be liable for the harm they cause.

If you require a background check, you should be able to justify the need for it and you need to not ask anything during the background check that you wouldn't ask an applicant directly. The background check should be given to all applicants for the particular position (don't check some and not others).

Using a consumer credit report for employment requires specific notices and disclosures. Don't even think about taking this route without the prior advice from a legal professional.

iv.   Doing pre-employment testing

 You may not require an applicant (or an employee) to pay the cost of a medical examination or the cost of furnishing any records required by you as a condition of employment. This applies to medical, physical, and drug testing.

1.   *Pre-employment Performance Testing*

In Minnesota, you can require performance-based testing before an applicant receives a job offer. The test cannot be used to discriminate against a protected class and it must:

- Measure only job-related abilities
- Required of all applicants
- Accurately measure the factors that are being tested

Employers who have 15 or more employees must also comply with the federal Equal Employment Opportunity Commission (EEOC) guidelines for pre-employment testing.

Like background checks, you should be able to justify the testing based on the essential job-related activities needed for the job. If the test isn't obviously related to the job, you may be using the wrong test or you may be testing when you shouldn't.

For the testing that you do use, you need to keep records of the testing, keep those records confidential, and actually use the test results as part of your hiring criteria, and administer and score the tests in a neutral, nondiscriminatory manner. The testing should be done in the same way and in the same environment for each applicant.

2. *Pre-employment Physical Testing*

You can require a pre-employment physical exam (including medical history) as a condition of employment if:

- There is an offer of employment contingent on passing the physical
- The physical only tests job-related abilities
- It is required of all people conditionally offered employment for that job
- The information regarding the physical and medical history is kept confidential as a medical record and kept separate from other personnel files

The one and only time you can ask a person about their physical conditions is during this exam.

You cannot refuse to hire someone based on their physical unless they are unable to perform the essential functions of the job. If you have 15 or more employees, you may be required to provide reasonable accommodations to the hire unless doing so would put an undue hardship on the company.

3. *When you can do drug or alcohol testing*

You can require a job applicant to take a drug/alcohol test if:

- You have a written drug/alcohol policy which complies with Minnesota law

- There is an offer of employment contingent on passing the drug/alcohol test
- The same test is required of all people conditionally offered employment for that job

You should require the person being tested to sign an acknowledgement that they read your drug/alcohol policy and that they understand that the offer of employment is contingent upon their passing the test. The testing must be done in a qualified laboratory and the applicant must be given an opportunity to list any medications or give an explanation for a positive test result.

You may withdraw a job offer if the person does not pass the drug/alcohol test.

v. Making the hire

1. *Employment Offers*

If you send a letter or email or other written communication offering employment, you don't want that to be taken for an employment contract. You should avoid making statements about looking forward to working with them for a long time, or anything that indicates that the relationship may be long term. If you are stating the amount of salary in the letter, either state it on a weekly basis, or state it on an annual basis with the caveat that the annual salary does not indicate employment for any specific term of time.

2. *Immigration Status*

Once you have hired someone, you are required to review their identity and work authorization documents and fill out a USCIS Form I-9 for that person. This is required of all employers, no matter what size the company is, and is required to be done on all hires, no matter if the person is a US born citizen. You are responsible for completing the second page on the form saving the completed form for three years from the date of hire or one year after the end of the employment, whichever is longer.

76

The fines for not complying are hefty. You can get the I-9 form on the USCIS website for free. Just do it.

    vi.   Hiring someone who's under someone else's non-compete agreement

Non-compete clauses are commonplace in employment contracts, and they are a vital shield for what might otherwise be a massive vulnerability to a company: the knowledge of the company's operations and trade secrets that its employees accumulate. A savvy (and sneaky) employee could be in a position to edge into the territory of his or her former employer, denying them significant revenues.

It is in the interest of both sides—former and new employer—that they avoid claims that could bring about costly court battles.

The best defense against any violations of non-complete clauses is prevention. Prevention starts with knowledge; after all, there's only so much you can do to defend against a threat you don't know is there. As you hire a new employee, ask about any previous employment contracts and insist on seeing the contract, then have your lawyer look for any non-compete clauses that could either land you in hot water or leave them incapable of performing the duties you expect of them.

You may have no intention of violating the non-compete provision, but new hires may not know what constitutes a violation of their previous contract and if you don't get clear about what is or is not a violation, the new hire may accidently violate the agreement and trigger liability or you. You must set out a clear line about what knowledge they carry with them from the former employer that they will be barred from using now. You want their skills and their personal contacts, but anything that may stem from confidential information puts your business at risk.

Before you hire, plan out your protection. Limit the terms of employment in their employment contract with you, and consider if the employee would be valuable enough to defend in court. If not, don't make the hire.

If you have weighed the risks and hired the employee, you may find yourself in a lawsuit. The cornerstone of your legal defense is documents. Documentation, whether paper, digital, or witnesses, provides your attorney something to point to as proof of no violation—or at least that any violation was not in bad faith. Anything that looks like a cover-up will only arouse suspicion. Negotiation with the employee's former company goes a long way towards leaving them reassured—and thus less likely to pursue litigation—and providing evidence of your efforts to avoid violation.

Say the worst has happened and you find your company on the defense in a court battle. Luckily, there's still reason to hope for a good outcome, especially if you've followed the above advice.

The former employer has plenty of room to slip up and invalidate the non-compete clause. If they failed to treat their confidential information as such, they have no legal ground to stand on if that information is used against them. The non-compete clause may also be unreasonably broad—lasting too long, lacking territorial limitation, etc. The court determines reasonableness on a case by case basis.

Also, if the former employer has breached the contract or failed to enforce non-compete agreements in the past, you may be in the clear.

Chapter 9: What rights do employees have?

These are the rights given to employees, whether they are full-time or part-time, or temporary or permanent.

a. Wages

As of the date of this writing, the Minnesota minimum wage is $9.65 for employers with gross annual sales of $500,000 or more, and $7.87 for employers with gross annual sales less than $500,000. People who earn tips do not get a lower minimum wage, and employers may not require workers to pool and share tips, although the workers are free to choose to do so.

Trainees, apprentices, student learners, interns, or whatever else you would want to call people coming in to work/learn get paid at least the standard minimum wage.

People with disabilities may be hired at less than minimum wage if the employer gets a permit from the Minnesota Department of Labor and Industries to do so. The wage may not be less than half of the standard minimum wage unless the employer has a permit from the US Department of Labor to pay less, and no more than 10% of a for-profit company's workforce may consist of employees with disabilities being paid less than minimum wage unless the company receives a special permit.

i. Overtime, maybe (exempt vs non-exempt employees)

Minnesota labor laws require employers to pay employees overtime at a rate of 1½ times their regular rate when they work more than 48 hours in a workweek (unless otherwise exempt under Minnesota's exemption rules), while federal law requires employers to pay employees overtime at a rate of 1½ times their regular rate when they work more than 40 hours in a workweek (unless otherwise exempt under the federal exemption rules), so for most businesses the overtime trigger is going to be 40 hours.

Whether someone is subject to overtime depends on whether they are non-exempt (will be subject to overtime) or exempt (not subject to overtime). The federal government and the state of Minnesota have similar, but not the same, criteria for exemption.

1. *Hours worked*

The amount employees should receive cannot be determined without knowing the number of hours worked, and you need to know what constitutes compensable time under the law.

The definition of "Employ" is "to suffer or permit to work." The workweek ordinarily includes all the time that an employee is required to be on the business' premises, on duty, or at a specific work place. "Workday" generally means the time between when an employee starts their "principal activity" and the time when they stop the principal activity or activities on any particular day. The workday can be longer than the employee's scheduled shift or scheduled hours.

Work that you did not request but "suffered or permitted" to be done is work time that you must pay for as the employer. For example, an employee may stay late to continue to work at the end of the day to finish a particular project. The reason they stay and work is immaterial; the hours they work are work time and are compensable.

Waiting time may be hours worked depending on the circumstances. Generally, if the employee was engaged to wait, it is work time; if the employee was waiting to be engaged, it is not work time. For example, a receptionist who reads a book while waiting for the phone to ring or an emergency room doctor who plays checkers while waiting for an emergency to come in is working during the periods of waiting. These employees have been "engaged to wait."

An employee who is required to be on call at your business' premises is working while "on call." An employee who is required

80

to be on call at home, or who is allowed to leave a message as to a number where they can be reached, is not working (in most cases) while on call. Additional limitations on the employee's freedom could require this time to be compensated.

Short rest periods, usually 20 minutes or less, are common in manufacturing and are paid for as working time. These short periods must be counted as hours worked. Unauthorized extensions of authorized work breaks are not to be counted as hours worked when you have clearly communicated to the employee that the authorized break may only last for a specific amount of time, and that extra break time is against your rules, and any extension of the break will be punished.

Actual meal breaks (usually 30 minutes or more) are not generally compensated as work time. The employee must be completely relieved from duty to eat their meal. If they are required to perform any duties, whether active or inactive, while eating, the employee was not relieved and must be paid for that time.

When an employee is required to be on duty for less than 24 hours and is permitted to sleep or engage in other personal activities when they are not busy, they are working even though they may be sleeping. When an employee is required to be on duty for 24 hours or more, they may agree to have regularly scheduled sleeping periods of not more than 8 hours taken out from their hours worked, provided adequate sleeping facilities are furnished by the business and the employee can normally get an uninterrupted night's sleep. No reduction in work hours is allowed unless the employee takes at least 5 hours of sleep.

If attendance at lectures, meetings, training programs and similar activities are outside of normal hours, voluntary, not job related, and no other work is concurrently performed, then the time is not counted. If all four criteria are not met, then the attendance is counted as working time.

The principles which apply in determining whether time spent in travel is compensable time depends upon the kind of travel involved. An employee who travels from home before the regular workday and returns to their home at the end of the workday (the regular daily commute) is not engaged in work time.

When an employee who normally works at a particular location is given a special one-day assignment in another city and returns home the same day, the time spent traveling to and from the other city is work time, except that you may deduct or not count the amount of time that the employee normally would have spent commuting to the regular workplace.

When an employee spends time in travel as part of their principal activity, such as travel from job site to job site during the workday, that time is work time and must be counted as hours worked.

Travel that keeps an employee away from home overnight is clearly work time when it encompasses the employee's workday. In this instance, the time is not only hours worked on regular working days during normal working hours, but also during the other hours on nonworking days during the away time. For example, if the employee is sent for a business trip that involves meetings on Friday and Monday and they do not return home for Saturday and Sunday, then their time away from home on Saturday is work time, as well.

Problems arise when employers don't realize that certain hours should be counted as working hours and fail to compensate for them. For example, an employee who stays at their desk while eating lunch and regularly answers the telephone and handles calls is working. This time must be counted and paid as work hours because the employee has not been completely relieved from duty.

2. *Non-exempt employees (they get overtime)*

There isn't a definition of non-exempt employees, except to say that a non-exempt employee is someone whose job description doesn't fit in any of the exempt employee types. The default is that a worker is a non-exempt employee, subject to wage and hour rules (minimum wage and overtime), unless the type of job they have is in one of the specific exemptions under Minnesota law or federal law.

3. *Exempt employees (they don't get overtime)*

a. Minnesota's criteria

Minnesota's exemptions apply to both minimum wage and overtime requirements. If the job fits the specific characteristics of one of the exemptions, then the minimum wage and overtime requirements don't apply to that worker. The job has to fit all characteristics of the type to qualify, and each type has a different test.

The exemption types include:

- Executive exemption
  - To qualify as an exempt executive employee, an employee must:
    - be paid a salary of at least $155 per week;
    - manage and supervise a department of at least two other full-time people (full-time is defined as at least 35 hours per week);
    - have authority to hire or fire or suggest changes to an employee's status;
    - regularly exercise discretionary powers, and;
      - either:
        - devote no more than 20 percent (40 percent if working in a retail or service establishment) to nonexempt work;
        - own 20 percent or more of the business; or
        - have sole charge of an independent or branch establishment.

- o An employee may also qualify for the executive employee exemption if he or she:
  - is paid a salary of at least $250 per week;
  - manages the enterprise or a recognized department or subdivision thereof; and
  - customarily directs the work of two or more other employees.
- Administrative exemption
  - o To qualify as an exempt administrative employee, an employee must:
    - be paid a salary or fee of at least $155 per week;
    - either:
      - perform office or nonmanual work directly related to business operations or management policies, or
      - administer an educational system or subdivision thereof in work relating to academic instruction;
    - regularly exercise discretion and independent judgment and makes important decisions;
    - either:
      - directly assist the business owner or a bona fide executive or administrative employee;
      - perform supervised work only along lines requiring special training or experience; or
      - execute special assignments;
    - devote no more than 20 percent (40 percent if working in a retail or service establishment) to nonexempt work;
  - o An employee may also qualify for the administrative employee exemption if he or she:
    - be paid a salary or fee of at least $250 per week;
    - either:
      - perform office or nonmanual work directly related to business operations or management policies, or

- - administer an educational system or subdivision thereof in work relating to academic instruction;
    - regularly exercises discretion or independent judgment.
- Professional exemption
  - To qualify as an exempt professional employee, an employee must:
    - be paid a salary or fee of at least $170 per week;
    - either:
      - perform work requiring advanced knowledge in a field of learning customarily acquired by prolonged specialized intellectual study, not a general academic education, an apprenticeship, or training in routine mental or physical processes;
      - perform original work dependent on their own creativeness in a recognized field of artistic endeavor; or
      - be a certified teacher working as such or recognized as such in a school system where they work;
    - consistently exercise judgment and discretion;
    - perform predominantly intellectual work so varied that the output cannot be standardized by time necessary for accomplishment; and
    - devote less than 20 percent of their hours worked to activities that are not essential to their professional work.
  - An employee may also qualify for the professional employee exemption if he or she:
    - be paid a salary or fee of at least $250 per week;
    - either:
      - performs work requiring advanced knowledge in a field of science or learning;

- performs work as a teacher in the activity of imparting knowledge; or
- performs work requiring invention, imagination, or talent in a recognized field of artistic endeavor;
  - consistently exercises discretion and judgment.
- Outside salesman exemption
  - To qualify as an outside salesman, an employee must:
    - make sales of, or obtain orders or contracts for, materials, services, or the use of facilities for which payment will be made;
    - make no more than 20 percent of all sales from the employer's place of business;
    - perform non-outside sales work no more than 20 percent of the time worked by non-outside sales employees.
  - Exempt work for outside salesmen includes incidental deliveries, collections, and other non-sales or non-solicitation work directly related to sales.

b. The Fair Labor Standard Act (FLSA) criteria

The federal exemptions are similar, but not the same, as the Minnesota exemptions and there are many more types than under Minnesota law. Under the federal exemptions, some jobs classify for an overtime exemption only (minimum wage still applies), and some jobs classify for both the exemption from minimum wage and overtime requirements. The most common exemption types are under the second type, and those are the only ones I have stated in full. If you have reason to need to look up any of the other exemption tests, you can find them at the Department of Labor's website at www.dol.gov.

Some job types are in both the overtime only exemption and the minimum wage and overtime exemption lists. The test for two

86

exemptions is different, and the worker will qualify for one or the other exemptions based on the situation in their particular position.

i. Overtime only exemption

Each exemption type has its own requirements that must be met for an employee to qualify for the exemption.

The types of exemptions from only the overtime requirements of the FLSA include motor carrier, rail carrier, outside dairy buyer, seaman, local radio and television station worker, motor vehicle dealership worker, watercraft salesman, driver and driver's helper on local deliveries, agricultural water access worker, livestock auction worker, county elevator worker, maple sap worker, produce worker, transportation of harvesters, taxicab driver, fire protection and law enforcement, domestic service, nonprofit educational institution, movie theater worker, forestry or lumbering operation worker, amusement or recreational establishment worker, and criminal investigator.

ii. Minimum wage and overtime exemption

Each exemption type has its own particular requirements that must be met for an employee to qualify for that exemption.

The most common types of employees that qualify for the federal exemptions for both minimum wage and overtime requirements include:

- Administrative Employees
  - For an employee to qualify for the administrative employee exemption, the following criteria must be met:
    - Earn not less than $455 per week;
    - be compensated on a salary or fee basis;
    - have the primary duty of performing office or non-manual work directly related to the management or

general business operations of the employer or the employer's customers; and

- as part of their primary duty, exercise discretion and independent judgment with respect to matters of significance.

- Computer Employees
  - To qualify for the computer employee exemption, all of the following tests must be met:
    - Earn not less than:
      - $455 per week on a salary or fee basis or
      - $27.63 on an hourly basis;
    - have the primary duty that consist of:
      - applying systems analysis techniques and procedures, including consulting with users, to determine hardware, software, or system functional specifications;
      - designing, developing, documenting, analyzing, creating, testing, or modifying computer systems or programs, including prototypes, based on and related to user or system design specifications;
      - designing, documenting, testing, creating, or modifying computer programs related to machine operating systems; or
      - performing a combination of the above-listed duties.

- Executive Employees
  - For an employee to qualify for the executive employee exemption, the following criteria must be met:
    - Earn not less than $455 per week;
    - be compensated on a salary basis;
    - have the primary duty of managing the employer's company or enterprise, or managing a "customarily recognized department or subdivision" of the company or enterprise;

- customarily and regularly direct the work of two or more other full-time employees; and
- possess the authority to hire or fire other employees, or the employee's recommendations as to the hiring, firing, advancement, promotion, or any other change to the status of other employees must be given "particular weight."

- Highly Compensated Employees
  - To qualify for the highly compensated employee exemption, an employee must:
    - have a total annual compensation of at least $100,000;
    - customarily and regularly perform one or more of the duties of an executive, administrative, or professional exempt employee;
    - Earn not less than $455 per week;
    - be compensated on a salary or fee basis; and
    - have a primary duty that includes performing office or non-manual work.

- Creative Professional Employees
  - To qualify as a creative professional for purposes of the FLSA minimum wage and overtime exemption, the employee must meet the following criteria:
    - Earn not less than $455 per week;
    - be compensated on a salary or fee basis; and
    - have the primary duty of performing work that requires invention, imagination, originality or talent in a recognized field of artistic or creative endeavor.

- Learned Professional Employees
  - To qualify as a learned professional for purposes of the FLSA minimum wage and overtime exemption, the employee must meet the following criteria:
    - Earn not less than $455 per week;
    - be compensated on a salary or fee basis; and

- have the primary duty of performing work that requires advanced knowledge in a field of science or learning that is customarily acquired by a prolonged course of specialized intellectual instruction.
- Teaching Professional Employees
  - The professional exemption applies to employees who:
    - have a primary duty of teaching, tutoring, instructing, or lecturing in the activity of imparting knowledge and
    - do so in an educational establishment.
- Outside Salesperson
  - For an employee to qualify for the outside sales employee exemption, the following criteria must be met:
    - have the primary duty of:
      - making sales, or
      - obtaining orders or contracts for services or the use of facilities;
    - customarily and regularly perform his or her primary duty away from the employer's place of business.

Additional types of exemptions from both the minimum wage and overtime requirements of the FLSA include amusement and recreational establishments, fishing operations, agricultural employees, small newspapers, switchboard operators, seamen, babysitters, domestic service employees, companionship services, and criminal investigators. Each of these types also have specific criteria to qualify for the exemption.

ii. Breaks

Minnesota labor laws require employers to provide employees restroom breaks and sufficient time to eat a meal. The meal time requirement applies to employees who work a consecutive shift of eight hours or more. If the break is less than twenty minutes long, that time must be paid. Additionally, the employer must give some time to use the restroom within each four consecutive hours of work.

iii.   Wage deductions

You may not deduct or withhold any part of an employee's wages for the following reasons, unless the employee has voluntarily consented to the deduction after one of these events has occurred or the employee has been held liable in court for the loss or indebtedness:

- cash shortages,
- lost or stolen property,
- damage to property,
- or any other claimed indebtedness running from the employee to you (the employer).

You may enter into a written contract with an employee in which the employee authorizes you to make payroll deductions for the purpose of paying:

- union dues,
- premiums of any life insurance,
- hospitalization and surgical insurance,
- group accident and health insurance,
- group term life insurance,
- group annuities or contributions to credit unions or a community chest fund, a local arts council, a local science council or a local arts and science council, or Minnesota benefit association, a federally or state registered political action committee, or
- participation in any employee stock purchase plan or savings plan for periods longer than 60 days, including Gopher state bonds.

You may make the following deductions from an employee's wages, so long as the employee's effective wage rate (how much they are paid after the deduction, per hour for that pay period) does not fall below minimum wage:

- purchased or rented uniforms or specially designed clothing required by the employer, by the nature of the employment, or by statute as a condition of employment, which is not generally appropriate for use except in that employment, not to exceed $50;
- purchased or rented equipment used in employment, except tools of a trade, a motor vehicle, or any other equipment which may be used outside the employment, not to exceed $50;
- consumable supplies required in the course of that employment;
- travel expenses in the course of employment except those incurred in traveling to and from the employee's residence and place of employment (the daily commute).

You must reimburse an employee for the full amount of any of the items listed above when the employee leaves your employment. You may, however, require the return of the uniform, equipment or other items.

b. Paid (and unpaid) leave

i. Sick leave

Minnesota law does not require employers to provide employees with sick leave benefits (either paid or unpaid). If you do choose to provide sick leave benefits, those benefits must comply with the terms of your business' established policy or the employment contract. Also, if you provide employees personal sick leave, you must also allow your employees to use their accrued sick leave to care for a sick or injured child.

You may be required to provide an employee unpaid sick leave in accordance with the Family and Medical Leave Act or other federal laws, and you are also required to comply with Minnesota's Parental Leave Act.

1. *Family Medical Leave Act (FMLA)*

The Family and Medical Leave Act (FMLA) applies to businesses who employ 50 or more employees and is designed to provide employees with temporary job security when faced with certain health-related care responsibilities for a family member that would prevent them from being able to work. Under FMLA, qualifying employees may have up to 12 weeks of unpaid leave for:

- Birth and care of the employee's child, or adoption or foster care placement of a child with the employee

- Care of an immediate family member (spouse, child, parent) who has a serious health condition

- Care of the employee's own serious health condition

For an employee to be eligible for FMLA, they must have worked at least 12 months for the employer (which do not have to be consecutive) and have worked at least 1,250 hours during the 12 months immediately before the date FMLA leave begins.

New provisions of the FMLA, included in the National Defense Authorization Act (NDAA), require an employer to provide up to 26 weeks of unpaid leave to the spouse, son, daughter, parent, or next of kin to care for a "member of the Armed Forces, including a member of the National Guard or Reserves, who is undergoing medical treatment, recuperation, or therapy, is otherwise in outpatient status, or is otherwise on the temporary disability retired list, for a serious injury or illness."

If you have an employee who is asking for FMLA leave, it is a good idea to get expert advice to help you navigate its complications.

2. *Minnesota Parental Leave Act*

Employees may take up to 12 weeks of unpaid leave upon the birth or adoption of their child when they work for a company with twenty-one or more employees, they have been with the company for at least 12 months, and they have worked at least half time during the past 12 months. The leave must be taken within 12 months of the birth or adoption and the employee must request the leave from you. The employee can choose when the leave will begin but you can adopt reasonable policies about when requests for leave must be made.

If you provide paid sick leave or paid vacation benefits, pregnancy or parental leave can count against that employee's paid leave so the total leave (parental plus paid leave) is not more than 12 weeks. The pregnancy or parental leave can also count against the employee's FMLA leave, as they only have a right to 12 weeks of leave total for birth or adoption of a child and any pregnancy related leave even if they qualify for both FMLA and pregnancy or parental leave. However, the employee may be entitled to additional leave under FMLA for a non-pregnancy related serious health condition.

If you provide health insurance benefits to your employees, you have to continue those benefits during the leave, but you may ask the employee to pay for this coverage. The employee must get their job back when they return from leave, and you cannot retaliate against your employee for requesting or taking the leave. Your employee is entitled to employment in their former position or one with comparable duties, hours and pay. They are also entitled to the same benefits and seniority they had before the leave. Also, they may return to part-time work during the leave without forfeiting the right to return to full-time work at the end of the leave.

ii. Vacation

You are not required to provide employees with any vacation benefits (either paid or unpaid). If you do choose to provide vacation benefits, though, those benefits have to comply with the terms of your business' established policy or employment contracts.

If your business does provide paid vacation benefits, you may establish a policy or enter into an employment contract that denies employees payment for accrued vacation leave when they leave employment. You can also establish a policy or enter into a contract disqualifying employees from payment for accrued vacation upon leaving employment if they fail to comply with specific requirements, such as giving two weeks' notice or being employed as of a specific date of the year. However, you are required to pay accrued vacation to an employee upon leaving employment if your business' policy or the employment contract requires it.

Neither Minnesota's legislature nor its courts have stated whether an employer is required to pay accrued vacation leave to an employee upon leaving employment if the business' established policy or the employment contract is silent on the matter.

You may cap the amount of vacation leave an employee may accrue over time, so long as the employees have signed contracts or written statements agreeing to that policy. You would likely be able to implement a "use-it-or-lose-it" policy requiring your employees to use their vacation time by a certain date or lose it, so long as the employee has agreed to the policy in writing.

iii. Holiday leave

Minnesota law does not require you to provide employees with holiday leave (either paid or unpaid). You can require an employee to work holidays and you do not have to pay an employee premium pay, (such as 1½ times the regular rate) for working on holidays, unless that time worked qualifies the employee for overtime under the standard overtime laws. However, if you do choose to provide either paid or unpaid holiday leave, that leave must comply with the terms of your business' established policy or the employment contract.

iv. Jury duty leave

You are not required to pay an employee any wages for time spent complying with a jury summons or serving on a jury, but you may not fire, threaten, coerce, or punish an employee for complying with a jury summons or serving on a jury.

v. Voting leave

Minnesota law requires that you permit your employees to take off, with pay, the time needed to vote in an election. An "election" is defined as "a regularly scheduled state primary or general election, an election to fill a vacancy in the office of United States senator or United States representative, or an election to fill a vacancy in the office of state senator or state representative." If you do not permit an employee to take paid voting leave as required by law, you are committing a misdemeanor. They take that seriously!

vi. Bereavement leave

Bereavement leave is leave that is taken by an employee due to the death of someone close to them, usually a relative. Minnesota law does not require you to provide your employees with bereavement leave or leave to attend funerals. You may, however, choose to provide bereavement leave and if you choose to do so, that leave needs to comply with your business' policy or practice on the matter.

c. Privacy

For all aspects of privacy where employers are "generally" allowed to monitor employees, it is best if you have a clear, written policy stated so that your employee doesn't have an expectation of privacy. Even if there is no specific prohibition on some of these aspects of surveillance, an employee could raise a claim of invasion of privacy under the common law (court-made case law) where a reasonable person would have an expectation of privacy in those circumstances. It would be better to not have to defend a lawsuit, whether or not you would have a right to act as you did.

i.   Email

As a general rule, employers may monitor an employee's email account that is provided by and maintained by the employer. That said, it would be much better for you to have a clear, written policy on the matter so that there would not be any expectation of privacy on the part of your employee.

For your employee's personal email account that may be accessed from the internet while they are at work, you have no right to access or monitor that account and doing so would open you up to both potential civil liability as well as potential criminal charges.

ii.   Phone

As a general rule, employers may monitor an employee's work phone that is provided by and maintained by the employer. That said, it would be much better for you to have a clear, written policy on the matter so that there would not be any expectation of privacy on the part of your employee. If you are monitoring the phone and realize that the call is a personal one, you need to stop monitoring for the remainder of that call.

iii.   Internet monitoring

As a general rule, employers may monitor an employee's internet use (browsing history) for a computer that is provided by and maintained by the employer, especially if that computer is only available and accessed during work hours. That said, it would be much better for you to have a clear, written policy on the matter so that there would not be any expectation of privacy on the part of your employee, particularly if that work computer is a laptop that may be taken home and used during non-work hours.

iv. Video surveillance

You may do video surveillance on your employee without warning as long as the video is not recording sound and the video is not done in areas where a person may be undressed (like in a locker room). You can do video surveillance without audio in a place where people are undressed if you put up a conspicuous warning sign.

v. Physical searches

There isn't any specific prohibition on physical searches (frisks, bag searches, desk searches), but this is an area where the court is most likely going to find on the side of the employee unless you have a compelling business reason to do the search and have communicated to the employee that they (or their bag or desk) would be subject to search in a clear, written policy. It would be even better to have a signed statement from the employee that acknowledges that they received a copy of the policy and have read it.

Physical searches are considered to be very invasive and trigger associations with unlawful searches in the law enforcement context. If you don't have a very good reason to be doing searches (like the workplace is a jewelry store or a bank), then just don't go there. If you do have a very good reason to be doing searches, work with a lawyer to create the right policy statement and procedure for doing the searches.

vi. Mail

It is a federal crime to obstruct the mail from being delivered to the person it is addressed to or to open someone else's mail and read it, subject to fines and up to five years in prison.

d. Severance Pay

Minnesota labor laws do not require you to provide your employees with severance pay. If you do choose to provide severance benefits, though, those benefits must comply with the terms of your business' established policy or the employment contract.

e. HR Records

You must allow all your employees access to their employment records. If you have twenty or more employees, then you are required to provide written notice of an employee's rights regarding their personnel file to new hires. You could have that notice be a separate document or it could be incorporated into your employee handbook, but either way it would be a good idea to have the employee sign a document that acknowledges that they have been provided a copy of the notice and have read it.

If an employee (current or former employee within a year of leaving) requests to see their personnel file, they have a right to see the file and you have seven business days to provide it (unless the record is stored out of state, in which case you have fourteen business days). The file must be made available during the employer's normal business hours at their normal workplace, but it doesn't have to be made available during the employee's normal work hours if those work hours are different than the normal business hours. You can have someone else present to monitor the employee reviewing their file.

Employees are entitled to review their records every six months (and former employees are entitled to review it once per year after they leave, so long as the records are maintained). After reviewing the file, the employee can make a written request to have a copy of the file (former employees can request the copy without reviewing it first, though). You cannot charge any fees for making the copies.

The personnel records that are available to the employee are limited and defined in the law. In the statute, personnel record means "any application for employment; wage or salary history; notices of commendation, warning, discipline, or termination; authorization for a deduction or withholding of pay; fringe benefit information; leave records; and employment history with the employer, including salary and compensation history, job titles, dates of promotions, transfers, and other changes, attendance records, performance evaluations, and retirement record."

It does not include reference letters, information regarding pending civil or criminal investigations, educational records, results of employer testing, information relating to the employer's salary or staff planning, written statements with personal information about someone other than the employee, written comments by the employee's supervisor or a company executive (if those records are only kept by the author and not put into the record), material that would be subject to a privilege (like an attorney-client privilege) in an administrative or judicial process, co-worker statements regarding the job performance or job related misconduct of the employee that identify the co-worker, and medical reports and records. The most likely of this list that you will have to deal with is the complaint from a co-worker. If an employee has something controversial in their file and requests access to it, it would be wise to have it reviewed by your lawyer to determine what should be given to the employee and what shouldn't.

Employees have the right to dispute items in their files and request that they be revised or removed. If you do not agree that the item should be revised or removed, the employee has the right to submit a written response up to five pages long to be included in his or her file, and their response must accompany the disputed information when it is ever accessed or given out.

You should not allow access to the employee's personnel file or reveal anything about it unless required to do so under the law or under compelling circumstances after getting advice from your lawyer.

You may not retaliate against your employee for asserting their rights regarding access to their personnel file.

f. The employment agreement

In Minnesota, employees are considered "at will" employees by default, meaning that you can let them go for any reason or no reason (provided it isn't one of the impermissible reasons, like discrimination) and they can quit at any time for any reason or no reason. The "at will" nature of the relationship can be altered by agreement of the employer and the employee.

i. At will, under contract, or both?

If you want something other than an at will arrangement with your employee, then you'll have to have an employment agreement. That agreement doesn't have to be in writing unless it cannot be fulfilled in a year; but even if it doesn't have to be in writing, it should be. Employment terms that alter the at will arrangement may be that the employee is guaranteed employment for a certain amount of time, or that they have to give some amount of notice before they quit, or that they can't be fired except "for cause".

If you send a letter or email or other written communication offering employment that you don't want to be taken for an employment contract, you should avoid making statements about looking forward to working with them for a long time, or anything that indicates that the relationship may be long term. If you are stating the amount of salary in the letter, either state it on a weekly basis, or state it on an annual basis with the caveat that the annual salary does not indicate employment for any specific amount of time.

You can have an employment agreement and still maintain the at will arrangement. In those cases, the purpose of the agreement is to delineate other aspects of the employment relationship, often to protect the employer. If you do want to have an employment agreement in place, then the timing of the agreement can make the difference between the agreement being enforceable, or not being worth the paper it is written on. As you may recall from Chapter 7, one of the requirements for a valid, enforceable contract is consideration, otherwise known as the bargained for exchange. If you hire someone and they start to work for you *and then* you bring out an employment agreement for them to sign, there isn't any bargained for exchange because you've already given them the job. For the employment agreement to be binding and enforceable, you must either 1) make their being hired conditioned on their signing the agreement and make them sign it before starting work or 2) pay them money (more than a nominal amount) as the bargained for exchange.

    ii.   A few important provisions in the Employee Agreement

      1. Non-compete

Non-compete agreements are generally disfavored and won't be upheld unless there is a compelling business reason to do so, and the agreement is reasonable as to its terms. This means that the more specialized or rare your product or service, the more compelling the reason to protect your business with a non-compete. What will be considered reasonable in the terms is going to be different from one business to the next, with some having a limited geographical scope and others warranting a global scope (although that would have to be really, really compelling). Likewise, what is reasonable as to time is going to be different from one business to the next, although the court has already ruled that one year is a reasonable amount of time for a non-compete (provided that one is warranted).

The factors that will be considered are the need to protect the business (general competition is not sufficient), the location of the business' customers and the locations where the employee worked with them, and the amount of time needed for the business to replace the employee, train the replacement, and allow the customers to get to know the replacement and forget about the former employee. In other words, the courts want to give the business a chance to hold onto its customers before the old employee can set up a competing business (or go to work for a competitor) in the same territory.

2. Non-solicitation

Unlike non-compete agreements, non-solicitation agreements are widely enforced. With a non-compete agreement, the business interests of the employer are being prioritized over the former employee's need to have a job, and courts don't like to keep people from working if they don't have to. On the other hand, non-solicitation agreements allow the former employee to work and they also protect the business.

A non-solicitation agreement states that the former employee cannot seek to do business with any current or recent past client of the employer for a certain amount of time, usually one to three years. In some agreements, if the clients want to follow the former employee, he or she can serve them and pay some percentage of the revenues to the former employer.

3. Performance

Performance aspects of an employment agreement are very specifically tailored on an individual basis, but can be very useful where an employer wants to make sure that a hire is going to be suitable for the job before committing long term. Often these terms are structured with a certain probationary period, or a series of probationary periods with increasing rights at each stage, until the person is considered a regular employee. Other uses for performance measures are in jobs where employees need to meet certain metrics to be worth the company's investment in them, like in sales.

g. The employee handbook

Technically, you don't have to have an employee manual. It is, however, an efficient way of giving all the employee workplace rights notices you are required to give, and having your additional policies stated in writing is a best practice. The employee handbook can save you from answering the same questions over and over, and better yet, from answering those questions differently each time. If you have a handbook that is up to date and you have documentation that records that employees acknowledge that they received it and have read it, then it even may provide legal protection for you if there is ever a lawsuit involving a situation in your workplace.

You may want to use disclaimers in your employee handbook to help keep you from having your employee handbook be considered an employment contract. Disclaimers must be clear and conspicuous; some good provisions to include in your disclaimers are:

- You retain the right to terminate the employment for any reason not prohibited by law and at any time.
- The employee retains the right to resign from employment at any time and for any reason.
- Any agreements to the contrary regarding employment must be in writing and signed by the owner (or an officer) of the company.
- The application, offer of employment letter, and employee handbook do not constitute an employment agreement and the employee handbook may be revised by employer at their sole discretion at any time.
- (If being issued for the first time) The employee handbook supersedes all previously issued policies.

i. Smart policies

Policies that are tailored to your business and stated in general terms are smart policies. You want the policy statements to be guidelines that are followed, not rigid rules that create a contractual obligation on your part. If you are going to offer benefits, the employee handbook is a good place to provide basic information about the benefits, referring the employee to the plan itself for specific details. The handbook is a good place to state the company's policies on vacation time, sick time, holiday time, and such. It's also a good place to set forth information that generally applies to everyone in the company, like attendance, workplace conduct, use of company equipment, and the like.

ii. Not-so-smart policies

Things that change frequently or things that only apply to a small sub-group of employees should not be put in the handbook. Information that changes frequently can be disseminated by notices and information that affects a small sub-group should be given solely to that group in a separate document.

If your company is not subject to certain government mandated benefits, like the Family Medical Leave Act, but your employee handbook references it, then you are stating that employees are entitled to those benefits. It is important that your employee handbook not make promises that you can't or don't want to make.

Employees always have the right to organize for purposes of engaging in "concerted activities" to advance their interests as employees, and its important that your policies not be seen to infringe on that right or discourage that kind of organization. Where you particularly have to be careful is in statements that prohibit employees from posting negative things about the company on social media. It's natural that you would want to keep company insiders from airing dirt on the company in public platforms. However, those policies often get companies in more hot water than whatever negative public impressions they are trying to curtail.

iii. Beware of ignoring policies!

Sometimes companies create policies as to how things are going to be run, in theory, and then in practice something else entirely happens. For instance, many employee handbooks have some ideal procedure for giving an employee three notices and an opportunity to correct their actions before they are fired, and then something happens and the employee is fired on the spot. The court has held that when you provide a procedure that gives someone some due process in the employee handbook, they are entitled to that process, even though they were not entitled to any process at all before you gave them the handbook. Whatever you have in your handbook, you have to follow it.

If you have some policy or process in your handbook that is not working for you, change it, reissue the handbook to everyone, get their signatures on the acknowledgment form, and then move on.

Chapter 10: Uncomfortable conversations (employee discipline and discharge)

It happens from time to time that someone just isn't a good fit. Or maybe they don't have the qualifications that they seemed to have when you interviewed them. Or maybe they make a habit of helping themselves to your cash drawer. Whatever the reason, eventually a situation will arise in which you'll have to discipline an employee or even let someone go.

a. Handling problem employees

"Problem employees" can come in many varieties. Some varieties are (relatively) easy to handle: if someone doesn't have the skills to do their job, either provide training or move them on; if someone steals from you, call the police and move them on. Uncomfortable? Yes. Hard to figure out? No.

The harder "problem employee" is the one who is qualified and generally does a good job, but who seems to be dysfunctional in your workplace. When that happens, you have to look and ascertain: is it the employee that's dysfunctional, or is it the workplace that is dysfunctional and the employee is being impacted by it?

There're two main things I want you to be on the lookout for – possible personal problems or mental illness (it's the employee who is dysfunctional) and workplace bullying (it's the workplace that is dysfunctional). If there's workplace bullying going on, it's not the employee who is the problem; it's the bully that is the problem.

Before I talk about possible personal problems and mental illness issues, I want to give you some insight to how pervasive workplace bullying is. According to the 2017 WBI U.S. Workplace Bullying Survey, 61% of Americans are aware of abusive conduct in the workplace, 19% of Americans are bullied, and another 19% witness it. Of the bullies, 70% of perpetrators are men and 61% of bullies are bosses. Of the people who are bullied, 60% of targets are women, 40% of bullied targets are believed to suffer adverse health effects, and 29% of targets remain silent about their experiences.

When people do speak up, 71% of employer reactions are harmful to targets, and 60% of coworker reactions are harmful to targets. Workplace bullying is a real thing, just like playground bullying was a real thing when we were kids. I encourage you to not tolerate it in your company, and instead set a high standard for respectfulness in workplace behavior.

Culture is everything in a company and it starts at the top and flows downward. Bring in people who train in communication, diversity, and firm culture. You can turn things around if you are proactive and committed to it. If you don't know who to call, drop me a line and I'll send you referrals.

Problem employees can arise outside of a bullying environment, too. When considering these situations as they arise, ask yourself, "Did the behavior that's a problem suddenly come up, or has this been a longstanding issue?" If it's a sudden problem, look at potential triggers to address (is there a new supervisor, do they have new subordinates, do they have newly added stressors, or do they have some personal or family issues going on), and be attuned to their concerns and be ready to take them seriously if they say they are being harassed or bullied.

If the behavior has been a longstanding issue, you may have a serious problem on your hands. Employees who create dysfunction and put others on edge reduce morale, kill productivity, and create a toxic work environment. Good people will quit and you won't be able to get them back.

If you think that an employee's behavior may be caused by mental illness issues, then from a legal standpoint that employee may have rights under the Family Medical Leave Act (if that applies to your workplace; you have 50+ employees) and/or under the Americans with Disability Act (if that applies to your workplace; you have 15+ employees).

From a personal standpoint, a bit of compassion can go a long way. A management style that criticizes and focuses on problems can be especially challenging for an employee with a mental health issue. On the other hand, a supportive management style that focuses on solutions and employee success can significantly contribute to the employee's well-being. Some tips for handling the situation effectively include:

- Communicate without judgment. Be self-aware that you may have assumptions and judgments about the employee or their behavior. While it is natural and human to have judgments, it is possible to put those aside and communicate without allowing them to influence the conversation.

- Consider your own emotional reaction. It is important to be aware of and manage your own reaction to an employee's performance or behavior at work.

- Be supportive and clear. You need to be especially supportive and clear when mental health issues, such as chronic stress, burnout, anxiety or depression are present.

- A supportive management style focuses on the intended outcomes rather than the problem, so the conversation feels more like a collaboration focused on a solution and less like criticism. For example, instead of saying "This memo is full of typos," you might say, "We need this memo to be free of typos. What do you need to make that happen?"

- Be precise in what you want to avoid ambiguity. For example, instead of saying, "Do not miss deadlines," you might say, "I need you to give me your work product before five o'clock on the day of the deadline. How can I help you to do that?"

- Relate issues to performance rather than personality. For example, instead of saying "You are being a burden to the team when you're late with your part of the report," you could say, "When your part of the report is not ready when the team is assembling the presentation, they miss out on having your contribution and they need to take more time to cover that part again."
- Highlight positive attributes first. This could include emphasizing an employee's value to the team, work ethic, and accomplishments.
- Acknowledge rather than agree. Rather than agreeing or disagreeing, try to get an understanding of the other person's point of view and acknowledge that understanding before offering your own opinion.

If you've ruled out bullying and you've ruled out personal problems and mental illness issues, what you are left with is simply a performance problem. If that is the case, an approach that is sensitive, positive and constructive can help the employee to feel valued and more motivated to perform. Here are some ideas to help make your management style more supportive:

- Read the book *Crucial Conversations* by Kerry Patterson.
- Work with the employee to create objective (as opposed to subjective) performance measures, focusing on specific tasks that are challenging for that employee. Avoid making a single employee feel picked on by doing this process with all employees annually and more frequently with those struggling to perform well. The intent is to use this process to support success, uncover difficulties, and develop solutions, which all employees can benefit from.
- When talking about difficult issues, be open to realizing that your management style or approach may be uncomfortable for some employees.

- When discussing work tasks, ask the employee if there is any other work they do that you are not aware of or acknowledging.
- Set a time frame to get together and assess how things are working (e.g. 1 to 2 weeks after the discussion).
- Acknowledge to the employee that the conversation may be uncomfortable, having it will help you gain a better understanding of how to provide support for the employee's long-term success in all aspects of their job.
- If successful, communicate praise and recognition for what the employee has accomplished. If not successful, clarify the next steps, which could be a modification of the work approach, an accommodation if the struggles are related to a disability, or beginning progressive discipline if necessary.

b. Deciding whether to discipline or discharge an employee

When problems arise, be sure to work out the whole story. Context matters, and you can't get the context if you don't have the whole picture. Be sure to discuss the situation with the employee, as well as third party observers, while withholding judgment.

As you are fact finding and getting the background on the situation, keep a written record to provide context to future issues. How you address the problem will best be tailored to the specific circumstances at play. Take time to reflect before deciding what to do.

No problem was ever solved by ignoring it, and employee issues are no exception. By addressing it, you put a fork in the road: either the employee will improve in specific, outlined aspects or further disciplinary measures will be taken. This warrants a face-to-face discussion and in doing so, seek a mutually-fulfilling resolution with clear, specific and actionable items that must improve and a plan in place for making that possible. Avoid ambiguous warnings.

Instead, coach the employee toward better outcomes and if necessary, enforce immediate but discrete consequences. Find out what support you can provide that will help the employee succeed.

Give the employee a short, specific time frame in which you expect to see results.

If the employee is reticent to take responsibility, defensive, and otherwise resistant, you may have to let them go if they don't come around.

c. How to effectively and compassionately fire someone

First of all, I believe that every person has an absolute right to be treated with dignity and respect. How you treat someone as you let them go makes an enormous difference in their sense of self-worth.

Before you endeavor to let someone go, ensure that your decision-making process has been thorough and well-documented. Take some time to analyze the legal risks of dismissal and the possible effects on the business.

When the time comes, sit the employee down with the relevant decision makers and immediately take ownership of the decision. Be clear and precise in explaining the rationale behind the dismissal. Be ready to answer whatever questions the employee might have.

Above all else, be kind and respectful. Try to frame the departure positively and offer them advice on how to constructively proceed to the next phase in their life. An aimless and angry employee is more likely to pursue legal action than one with a goal for the future.

d. When do they get unemployment benefits?

An employee who has earned a certain minimum amount in the last year may qualify for unemployment benefits if they are unemployed "through no fault of their own." Generally, this means layoffs, but it also can apply to when an employee quits, if the reason they quit is because of some reason that is outside of their control, like due to a serious illness, cut in hours or pay, or their job moved.

When the former employee files an unemployment claim, you will be notified and given an opportunity to respond as to why the former employee should not be eligible for benefits. The former employee is not eligible for benefits if they were fired because of their misconduct, they quit without good cause, they failed to accept suitable work, they refused an offer of reemployment, or they participated in a labor strike. While it sounds black and white, there is actually plenty of grey area and its important to assemble all the documents and facts that you can when someone makes a claim, if in fact there are good grounds to contest it.

e.   **The last paycheck**

i.   When the employee is fired, terminated, or laid off

When you discharge or lay off an employee, you must pay the employee all wages due to them within 24 hours of the employee's demand for payment. If the employee was entrusted with collecting, disbursing, or handling money or property of the business, you may take ten calendar days after the separation from employment to audit and adjust the accounts of the employee before the employee's wages or commissions are paid.

ii.   When the employee quits or resigns

When an employee quits, you must pay the employee all wages due by the next regularly scheduled payday. If the next regularly scheduled payday is less than five days after the employee quits, you may pay the employee on the second regularly schedule payday after the employee quits or within 20 days, whichever is sooner. If the employee was entrusted with collecting, disbursing, or handling money or property of the business, you may take ten calendar days after the separation from employment to audit and adjust the accounts of the employee before the employee's wages or commissions are paid.

iii. Wage disputes upon separation

If there is a dispute between you and the employee as to the amount of wages due upon their leaving employment, you must pay the undisputed portion of the amount due on time.

f. Avoiding the most common employment litigation issues

When employees are terminated, sometimes they come back and sue. These are the most common reasons terminated employees sue.

i. Discrimination

To win on a discrimination claim, the employee must show that they were treated differently because of their age, sex, race, disability, national origin, etc. (the protected classes). To reduce the risk of losing a discrimination suit, you need to be able to show that your actions followed your business' policies and procedures and that the decisions made in this case were consistent with the actions that were taken in other cases with other employees who were not of that protected class.

ii. Breach of contract

Even though Minnesota is an "at will" employment state, a terminated employee may try to bring a breach of contract suit, saying that there was some agreement that prevented them from being let go as they were. If you have an employee handbook and it outlines a procedure for discipline and discharge and you followed that procedure, then there shouldn't be an issue. To reduce your risk of losing in this case, document the step by step procedures taken with the employee during the discipline and discharge

114

process and make notes of the conversations while they are happening, or shortly thereafter, so you have a complete written record that supports your position.

iii.   Whistleblower

To have a whistleblower claim, an employee has to make a report of a suspected violation of the law to either the employer or a government agency, and then the employer took an adverse action against them (i.e. they were fired). The best way to avoid this claim is to research whether or not the employee made any report before they are let go.

iv.   Retaliation

A retaliation claim arises when an employee engages in "a protected activity" (i.e. makes a complaint to the employer), and the employer retaliates by disciplining or discharging the employee. If the employee can show that their action caused the discipline or discharge, then they likely win. If you can show that they were disciplined for specific reasons that had nothing to do with the protected activity, then you likely win. To reduce your risk of losing in this case, document the problems that were arising in the employee's work product or whatever else was the source of the reason for them being let go, and document the step by step procedures taken with the employee during the discipline and discharge process and make notes of the conversations while they are happening, or shortly thereafter, so you have a complete written record that supports your position.

v.   Defamation

Defamation claims are very common and can be tricky to defend. Any negative statement about the employee that is shared within the organization can be the source of a claim. To lessen the risk, only allow those who have an absolute need to know receive communications and information during the fact finding and decision-making process.

Chapter 11: Independent Contractors

Many small businesses use independent contractors to perform critical operations like website development, marketing, bookkeeping and other important work that keeps the business functioning and growing. It's one of the best ways that a small business can stretch its budget to get everything done that needs to get done.

a. Why businesses love them (and the state and feds don't)

When a business uses an independent contractor, they don't have to pay the employer side Federal Insurance Contributions Act (FICA) tax because they don't handle payroll tax withholding, they don't have to pay unemployment insurance premiums, they don't pay worker's compensation for independent contractors, and independent contractors are not subject to the wage and hour laws (like overtime). Businesses can spend about 30% less for the same work by using an independent contractor. That is why businesses love using them.

The state and the federal government, however, do not love for businesses to use independent contractors. The reasons for this are two-fold. First, there is a compelling public policy reason for the wage and hour laws that have been created to make sure that workers are fairly compensated for the time they work, and an independent contractor arrangement circumvents those laws. Second, income tax revenues are most consistently collected and remitted by employers and it is those revenues that keep the government running, while tax payments from independent contractors are notoriously inconsistent.

Independent contractors, as small businesses themselves, are responsible for their own income tax reporting and remitting. There is a higher chance of underreporting on the part of the independent contractor that is not going to happen with employee payroll reporting, and there is also the likelihood that the independent contractor will not have put aside their portion of the tax liability from their pay, and will not consistently or even timely remit their tax payment. If everyone submitted their taxes like independent contractors do, as opposed to how employee payroll is handled, the government would run out of money trying to get everyone to pay up.

For these reasons, the state and the feds are not thrilled to have businesses use independent contractors in lieu of employees and have set forth specific tests designed to delineate who should be an employee, and who may be an independent contractor.

b. It's not enough to just sign an agreement

If you are working with an independent contractor, having a signed Independent Contractor Agreement is a very good idea, especially if that person is producing any work that has intellectual property rights (like working on your website or creating your marketing materials), or interacting with your customers, or having access to your client data. That agreement is not the final say, though, as to whether that person may be an independent contractor or if they should be an employee as far as the state and federal government are concerned.

If a controversy arises regarding the status of a worker, it will be settled based on the balance of the factors listed below, and the written agreement will be just one factor to be considered. If you want to make sure that you stay in the clear, make sure your independent contractor relationships check most, if not all, of the boxes. Otherwise, you would be better off making that person an employee, even if just part-time or on a temporary basis.

Independent Contractor Tests:

Common Law Agency Test:

- ☐ Does the hirer control the manner and means by which the end product is achieved?

- ☐ Does the hiring party have the right to assign additional projects?

- ☐ Does the hirer control the schedule of the hired?

- ☐ Does the hired have control over hiring and paying his assistants?

- ☐ Does the hired receive the means of his work from the hirer?

- ☐ Does the hired already possess the skills required?

- ☐ Does the relationship between the hirer and hired endure beyond completion of the initially established project?

Economic Realities Test:

- ☐ Does the hirer control the manner in which the work is performed?

- ☐ Does the hirer have a task needing a specific skill?

- ☐ Does the hired base his business around the skill required?

- ☐ Does the hired operate with their own equipment and assistants?

- ☐ Does the working relationship endure past completion of the project?

The simplest way to support your classification of a worker as an independent contractor is to maintain a set of documents that establishes their unquestionable qualification for the categorization.

Here are just some of the means by which you can do so. Remember, the more, the better!

- ☐ A Minnesota business license in the name of the worker's business
- ☐ A list of the worker's other customers, with work agreements
- ☐ Photographs of advertisement for the worker's business
- ☐ A list of the worker's employees
- ☐ Testimony from the worker explaining the relationship
- ☐ The worker's independent website or white pages listing
- ☐ The worker's accounting books and records

c. A few important provisions in the Independent Contractor Agreement

I don't want you to get the impression from the previous section that an Independent Contractor Agreement isn't important; it is. Documenting the relationship with a written agreement is still useful; it helps to delineate the terms under which you are both agreeing to operate. And depending on what the independent contractor is doing for you, you may be leaving yourself at significant risk if you don't have a written agreement with some key terms.

i. Work for hire

The default setting for intellectual property is that the person who created the work owns the rights to that work. There is another default setting for intellectual property that says when an employee creates something in the course of his or her employment, the created work belongs to the employer. In the case of an independent contractor, as previously discussed, they are not employees and you are not their employer. Therefore, the intellectual property rights for the work they create belong to them, even though you are paying them to create the work.

What can happen is that the relationship with the independent contractor can turn sour, and then that person can insist that you stop using all those works that he or she created for you. For you to continue to do so would be a copyright infringement, and you can be on the hook for huge damages if you willfully violate someone's copyright.

The way to protect yourself is with a "work for hire" agreement which can be built right into your independent contractor agreement. Under a work for hire agreement, the intellectual property rights belong to you instead of the independent contractor.

ii.   Confidentiality

If the independent contractor is going to be working with your client data, proprietary systems and processes, or anything that would be classified as a trade secret, then you'll want a confidentiality clause built into the independent contractor agreement.

iii.   Non-solicitation

If the independent contractor is going to be working with either your clients or your employees, then you will want to protect your business by preventing them from soliciting your clients for their own gain or for the benefit of another company, and preventing them from recruiting your employees for their own company or for another company with a non-solicitation clause built into the independent contractor agreement. Non-solicitation is different than a non-compete clause, and is more readily upheld by the court as a necessary protection for a business. The independent contractor can still go out and get work that is competitive with yours or work with your competitors, they just can't take your clients or your employees when they do.

iv.   Tax handling

Although the tax handling aspect of an independent contractor arrangement is apparent in the nature of the relationship, it is still a good idea to state it explicitly so there are no misunderstandings or unmet expectations.

At a minimum, the tax clause should address that the independent contractor will be responsible for all withholding and deductions for all taxes (including income taxes, FICA, and Medicare taxes), unemployment insurance, and workers compensation insurance, and other similar taxes, and payroll expenses, and that they will also be solely liable for all taxes based on their net or gross income. There should be a statement that the independent contractor will indemnify the business (reimburse it for any liability) from his or her failure to make those tax payments.

v.   Liability indemnification

The independent contractor's liability indemnification may be made to extend beyond the tax payment liability in the previous section. Other important areas of indemnification may be for any liability the business may receive based on intellectual property (including trade secrets) brought to the business by the contractor, liability based on any violation of an employment agreement with someone else (non-compete agreement), and liability based on the contractor's negligence or causing harm that is brought by the business' clients, vendors, or employees.

d.   The perils of misclassification

The consequences of misclassifying an employee as an independent contractor can be severe, particularly if you acted in full knowledge of the error. Here are just a few potential outcomes for the business:

- Payment of unpaid Social Security, Medicare tax, unemployment tax, and income tax.
- Payments of fines and interest for not paying the above, as well as fraud.

122

- Exposure to criminal and civil lawsuits from both the government and employee.
- Contractor reclassified as employee, and payment of back pay for overtime (if applicable).

Each one of these items can be very expensive on their own, and cumulatively they can be enough to make your business go under. Plus, once you are on their radar, your business can expect to have regular audits of your tax, payroll, and employee records. If they have reason to believe that there could be additional violations, they will come and search them out.

Chapter 12: Filling the coffers
(raising money and bringing in investors)

Companies can't get off the ground without funding, and not everyone has a stash of money set aside to seed their business. For most business owners, this means raising money through a variety of means.

a. Self-funding

Even if a business owner is going to turn to outside sources for funding, a certain amount of their own money is going to go into their business. That portion is what we call self-funding. That funding may come from savings or from personal lines of credit and credit cards. Whatever you put into your business, you need to keep track of it as either capital contributions or loans to your business.

I do not recommend that you borrow against or cash out your 401(k) or IRA account to fund your business. First of all, the early withdrawal penalties and taxes will take a significant cut. Second, as long as you leave those accounts untouched, your business can go down in flames, you can declare bankruptcy, and those accounts will come through the process wholly untouched and intact. If you take the money out (and get only a fraction of it after penalties and taxes), and put it towards your business and things don't work out, you have lost that money.

I know you are committed to your business. I know you are "all in." I just don't want you to jeopardize your retirement plans just yet.

b. Getting corporate credit

If you do things right, you likely won't have to crack open your IRA (like I was warning you about) when your business runs short on cash. Once you have your business entity set up and get your federal tax ID number (FEIN), you can start to get credit established for your business. Remember that as long as you are not a sole proprietor, your business is an entity that is separate from you. Therefore, it can have a credit score that is separate from yours.

Unlike people, who end up with a credit score whether they want one or not, businesses actually have to be proactive about establishing a credit score to get one. Actually, a business can be extended a line of credit and diligently pay on it and never get the benefit of it if they haven't gone to register their business in the system. The business' system for credit is maintained by Dun & Bradstreet, and you start establishing your business' credit by registering for a D-U-N-S number (it's free). Go on their website and click the link for "Get a DUNS number."

Just because you got a DUNS number for your business doesn't mean that your business has credit separate from you just yet. When your business is new (or when your business isn't new but it hasn't had its good payment history recorded anywhere), no one knows whether it is credit worthy or not, and so they will rely on your credit score to extend credit to your business. When they do this, the lendability is determined by your credit, but the amount of credit extended to your business is not reported on your credit. Once your business has established a good credit history, then it will qualify for financing on its own without your credit score to bolster it up. It may take a year or more, but if you are quite intentional, you can get there much sooner.

The best thing you can do is to have a real website, and a real email address (so&so@realwebsite.com) instead of an @gmail.com or @yahoo.com email, which increases your legitimacy and will increase your initial score. Put these things in your DUNS profile. Then have a bank account for your business, in the name of the business, with the business' FEIN. Then go and get a small line of credit in your business' name (making sure that it is a company that is reporting to Dun & Bradstreet). A gas credit card is a good option. If you can get a few small lines of credit going, even if you

126

have to use your personal credit score to start, you will start to build that credit score.

Then, from time to time, stop in to the bank where your business' bank account is and ask the commercial banker to see if they will give your business an open line of credit. An open line of credit is a nice thing to have when you're in business. It is money that is quickly and easily available to you when you need it, but you don't pay interest on it until you borrow it. Then when your business is short on cash, you can turn to your line of credit instead of your IRA.

You need to do this process sooner than later. For one thing, it takes time to build the score. For another, many business owners take a hit on their personal credit at some point early on in business ownership. If you try to do this process when your personal score isn't high enough to get approved for credit, it will be a bit harder for you to get started. If you're not personally lendable, then neither will your business be.

Once your business has well established credit, it will be able to get financing on its own, and that can also help to make your business a valuable, saleable asset.

c.   SBA loans

The US Small Business Administration (SBA), which is an agency of the US government, has a ton of great resources for small business owners. Their website is full of educational resources (www.sba.gov), plus they are the ones who have the SCORE program, which matches small business owners with retired business owners and executives for mentoring and consulting for free. It's a great program and you should check it out, especially if you have been thinking that you could use some guidance but can't afford a business coach (www.score.org/find-mentor).

The SBA has a loan program in which a partner bank lends money to a small business, and the SBA guarantees the loan. If the small business goes under, the bank isn't left holding the bag, so it makes banks more willing to lend to small businesses. Like anything with the government, though, there are qualification requirements and a bit of red tape.

The first step is contacting a qualified lender, although it is easy to do. Just google "Minnesota SBA lender" and you'll have plenty of choices come up. Next, you put in the application with the lender and it goes through their underwriting process. Then, if the bank approves your application, it goes off to the SBA for final approval. And then, you get your financing. It sounds simple, and it can be, but it's not always fast.

Not every type of business qualifies for an SBA loan, and there are limitations on what you can do with the money. The business owner does have to have creditworthiness. You cannot have a defaulted student loan, or be behind on a government backed mortgage, or have a recent felony on your record.

For businesses that qualify, the SBA loan can be a lifesaver. It's worth at least having the conversation with your banker to see if its an option for you.

d. Working with investors

In order to offer an equity share of your business in exchange for money, you have to be compliant with the Securities and Exchange Commission (SEC) regulations. If you think that sounds scary, that's because it is. You hear stories in the news about people going to prison for SEC violations, although in reality it is usually for securities fraud (like Bernie Madoff) or insider trading (like Martha Stewart). The likelihood of a small business owner being sent to the pokey for getting aunt Edna to invest in her company is virtually non-existent, but technically it could happen. An investment is a security, and regulated by the SEC, if money is taken in exchange for equity of a business that someone else is running. If aunt Edna has no voting rights in the company, it's a security. However, if aunt

128

Edna does have voting rights, then she's just a co-owner, like you are, and that isn't a security. Only sales of securities that are not in compliance with SEC regulations are a problem; if the deal is structured so that it isn't a security, the SEC has nothing to do with it.

If you want aunt Edna to invest, and you don't want her to have voting rights in the company, there's a type of security offering that you can do that's called a private placement. In a private placement, you don't register the offering with the SEC like you do with a public offering, and you don't have to do the prospectus and all the other legal and financial wrangling that you have with a public offering. You are, however, limited to offering the investment only to people you know and are connected with and who are "accredited investors." An accredited investor is a person who either has an excess of $1 million in assets (excluding their primary residence) or who made $200,000 per year for the past two years (or $300,000 jointly if married). So, if aunt Edna is a high-income earner, a private placement might just be the thing to do.

The other option for friends and family to invest is to lend money to the company, as debt, instead of buying shares of the company, as equity. When friends and family members do this, they are earning the interest on the loan and providing the capital the business needs. Loans aren't a security, so the SEC doesn't care about them at all.

If the business takes off and does well, the equity investors will reap the most reward and the debt investors will only get paid back what they were supposed to get paid back. If the business fails, the equity investors will lose their money, and the debt investors will be in a better position to collect from the liquidation as creditors. If you ever have the opportunity to work with a venture capital firm or angel investors, you'll see that some favor venture capital (equity buys) while others favor venture debt (private loans).

e. Crowdfunding

Crowdfunding websites used to only allow you to essentially pre-sell a product (or conceivably a service) during development, but since the JOBS Act was introduced in 2016, a company can raise up to $1 million in 12 months using equity crowdfunding. For equity crowdfunding, the crowdfunder has to be approved by the SEC; you can find that list at www.finra.org/about/funding-portals-we-regulate.

If you choose to go the route of equity crowdfunding, be sure you are comfortable sharing your financials with strangers and be prepared to answer some tough questions about how your company is doing and its potential for growth.

f. Other various sources of funding

If you have bad credit but your business still needs financing, there are some options available, but they are expensive and you should use them only as a last resort. If you have regular revenues coming in through your credit card processing, you may be able to get a merchant advance loan. They provide you with a lump sum of cash, and then they take a certain payment amount out of your bank account every day. The terms of payment are set in advance and you have no savings on interest if you pay it off early.

The other option is hard money lenders. A hard money lender isn't lending on your credit score, they're lending on the collateral you put up, most often a business' commercial real estate. Usually the loan to value ratio is 70%, meaning you will get a loan for 70% of the value of your collateral, but lose 100% of it if you default. Hard money lenders are quick to foreclose if you default, so if you are going to do a deal with a hard money lender, don't default.

Chapter 13: Protecting the nest egg (insurance, financial management, legal maintenance, and tax matters)

Provided that you have a good service or product, the best way to have your business have longevity is to have its insurance, financial systems, legal matters, and tax matters handled without any gaps between them. Why? Because it's from those areas that unexpected catastrophe may befall a business, when there are gaps. When a business has a solid foundation in these areas, it helps to make it a valuable, saleable asset. In fact, when I assist a business owner sell their business, these are exactly the areas from which most of the seller's due diligence comes from.

a. Insurance

Insurance is one of the most important investments you can make in your business, but one that many people overlook.

i. What kind?

What kind of insurance you need depends on your business. Here are some of the most common types that a business may need:

- General business liability – for coverage of the businesses' "stuff" and liability in case of personal injury
- Commercial real estate – for coverage of the building that the business owns
- Errors and omissions (a.k.a. professional liability) – for coverage on mistakes in work
- Product liability – for damage caused by a dangerous or defective product
- Cybersecurity – for loss caused by computer hackers
- Cargo insurance – for loss of goods in transit from the factory
- Umbrella – for extra coverage for anything so that the business owner's personal assets are not at risk

One of the important aspects of commercial insurance is working with someone who specializes in commercial insurance. The person who handles your homeowner's and auto policy may tell you that they can handle your business insurance, but unless they actually have been writing several hundred commercial policies per year, they are unlikely to provide you with the best advice. Commercial insurance policies are extremely detailed and technical, and what appears to be a small thing in a dense contract can completely exclude you from coverage when some specific thing happens differently than expected. For instance, I have a client who had what appeared on the surface as a decent products liability policy. He had a product fail, and it caused some economic loss to his customer, so he turned it in to his insurance carrier. It wasn't covered because the policy was written only for physical harm to a human being, and not economic loss because the thing didn't work. In other words, if it had exploded, it would have been covered. The fact that it didn't, meant that it wasn't.

ii. How much?

There's a balancing point for the just right amount of insurance. If you're underinsured, then you're leaving yourself exposed to risk, and that's going to cost you eventually. If you're overinsured, then you're paying too much in premium for benefits that you'll never receive (insurance coverage on everything except life insurance is based on the value of the loss or claim, not what the coverage limits are). Finding the sweet spot where the insurance amount is right to cover the potential loss or claim without grossly being overinsured is where you want to aim.

b. Financial Management

The financials are the vital signs of the company. How can you know if it's on the verge of crashing if you don't know the status of the financials? Being busy isn't enough; having cash coming in isn't enough; you need to know that you have more coming in than going out, when, and how much. Companies with tight financials (they are on top of their numbers) are worth more than companies with the same or similar product or service and the same amount of revenues that have slipshod books because the ability to manage by the numbers in real time is so valuable.

i. Maintaining the books

Unless you have a bookkeeping business, doing your books is one of the first things you should outsource. Many business owners are simply too busy to fit doing the books in, hate doing it and put it off, and then can't remember what the details of transactions were because it was too long ago by the time they get around (read: have to) get the books caught up. Why torture yourself? A bookkeeper costs in the ballpark of $60-80 per hour, can do your books in a fraction of the time that you can, and if you allow them to keep on top of it, then your books will be ready at a moment's notice. This is helpful for your taxes and getting business financing, but it is imperative if you are going to manage your business by the numbers. Plus, the tax savings from the entries that you couldn't remember well enough to log properly when you were doing it yourself some months after the transaction will cover the cost.

ii. Knowing your numbers

Every business has certain metrics that are key to measuring its success, and all businesses have some metrics in common that everyone recognizes as being crucial indicators of success. Just knowing the number, in isolation, isn't enough. Is $1 million in sales good? Maybe, maybe not. Is it good in relation to what? If your sales are $1 million but your expenses are $2 million, $1 million in sales now doesn't sound so hot. Likewise, if your sales are $1 million, but last year's sales were $10 million, $1 million doesn't sound all that impressive.

It's important to know your numbers and to also be able to see them in context. You need to be able to see how all the numbers in any given reporting period interplay, and you need to be able to see how the numbers are trending over time.

Also important is to get a handle on the key indicator numbers for your particular business. You may not know what those are at the beginning, but over time you will start to notice correlated trends. For instance, you may notice that when you track phone calls, that for every 100 calls you make to prospects, you make an additional $1,000 in sales. There are things to keep an eye on (and to keep a count on) other than just dollars. When you start to get really interested in why you have certain upticks in business and why you have certain slumps, and start to observe what is going on immediately preceding those events, you'll start to get a sense for the types of numbers I'm talking about.

Once you know what the key indicators of success are for your business, you'll know what you need to do to push those numbers up, and your success will naturally follow.

iii. Managing by the numbers (not the feelings)

If you have the observational and tracking systems in place that naturally arise from the process that I just described in the above section, you will be in an excellent position to see the impact of things that otherwise would have been lost. When you can make those connections, you can see what to do more of and what to do less of; you're not guessing about what is effective. When you can manage by the numbers, you'll be operating with much, much more confidence. When people "hope" that things work, they are managing on feelings. Hope is wonderful for the holidays, but it makes a lousy business plan.

c. Legal Maintenance

Setting up your business right is only the first step. Keeping your business legally up to date and in check is an ongoing task that needs to be handled from time to time, no less than annually.

i. Staying on top of legal regulations

Some businesses are in industries with many legal regulations that are swiftly changing, while others are in industries that haven't changed since the fax machine was invented. Industries with swiftly changing legal landscapes that I've worked with in the recent past include home health care, adult day care, and medical marijuana. For business owners in those industries, and the legal counsel that advise them, it is very important to keep a finger on the pulse of regulatory changes and make sure they stay in compliance. Even for businesses that are in industries with infrequent changes, keeping on top of regulations is still important because the regulatory landscape of business in general tends to shift over time.

Regardless of what industry a business is in, it still has to satisfy the minimum regulatory requirement of renewing its business with the Secretary of State's office for the state(s) in which it is registered.

ii. Staying on top of your corporate recordkeeping

At a minimum, a corporation must have an annual meeting, and that meeting must be recorded in the corporation's records. A partnership (LP, LLP, LLLP) and a limited liability company (LLC) are not required to have an annual meeting, unless required by the partnership agreement or the operating agreement, but it is a good idea that they do, nonetheless. Keeping up to date on the corporate record book helps to ensure that the personal liability shield that the entity provides stays in place in case of a lawsuit or creditor claim.

If at any point in the future you want to sell your company, it is truly a nightmare to reconstruct a business' corporate record book across many years. Believe me, I've done it many times, and it ends up being costly to do with only a fraction of the important detail as it would have had the records been kept contemporaneously.

iii.   Checking in as you grow

As your business grows, it is important to make adjustments for risk allocation and overall efficiency. The legal aspects of your business shouldn't be "set it and forget it." The right structure for your business at one stage of its growth may not work as well when it is ten times the size, or with multiple investors, or with business across several state lines. As your business evolves, so should your legal systems.

d. Tax Matters

I advise that you work with a CPA who focuses their practice on serving business owners. That doesn't mean that they wouldn't do your personal return as well, but it does mean that they really know the nuances of the tax code as it relates to business. (Not a dabbler)

I recommend that you have a meeting with the CPA at least two times each year, if not more depending on your business. During tax season, your CPA will be up to his or her eyebrows in tax returns and will not have the time nor mental bandwidth to talk to you about possible tax saving strategies, and even if they could, it would be too late to implement any decent strategy. The meeting during tax season is solely for the purpose of reviewing your return for accuracy, getting your questions answered, signing the authorization to file electronically, and most importantly, bringing your CPA a caffeinated beverage and some chocolate.

The other meeting should take place in late September or early October and the purpose of that meeting is to talk about potential tax saving strategies. At this point in the year, you'll have a good sense of what the end of year profit is targeted to be and you'll be in a good position to move that number up or down depending on your goal for that year's reporting. If you're trying to get a business loan, or to get a mortgage, or get ready to sell your business, you are going to want all the profit you can muster on that tax return. If you're not trying to do any of those things, you likely want to reduce your profit as much as possible to save on taxes.

Tax strategies for increasing profits in the reporting year include pre-selling goods or services in the current year to be delivered the following year, provided you operate on a cash basis (and not accrual). You can also push up profits by raising prices in the last quarter. Keep in mind that an increase of 4% will generally be accepted, and anything more than that may be met with customer complaints or lost sales.

You can also push up profits by offering something new to your current clientele in the last quarter. If you own your business' building, you may be able to push up profit by using a cost segregation service (cost segregation is the process of separating out the non-real estate property that is tied to a piece of real estate and putting those items on a different expense/depreciation schedule from the real estate itself).

Tax strategies for decreasing profits include making a fourth quarter purchase of equipment that you otherwise would have purchased the following year, pre-purchasing the supplies needed in the first quarter of the following year, prepaying on services and utilities that you'll use in the first quarter of the following year, prepaying office rent, and giving generous end of year bonuses to employees. A tax strategy for decreasing your personal income liability include contributing the maximum allowed amount into your traditional IRA and Roth IRA.

Your CPA no doubt will have many more strategies, but you'll never know unless you make the appointment and go see them at the start of the fourth quarter.

i. The power of tax savings

"The legal right of a taxpayer to decrease the amount of what otherwise would be his taxes, or altogether avoid them, by means which the law permits, cannot be doubted." From the legal opinion of the United States Supreme Court, Justice George Sutherland writing in *Gregory v. Helvering.*

In this country, we have the right to use legal means to reduce our tax burden. I happen to be liberally minded and I personally believe that it is every citizen's duty to provide their share to make our society a safe, clean, educated and healthy one.

I also happen to know that paying too much in taxes can stunt the growth of a small business (or a family's wealth) to such an extent that that business (or family) is unable to make the positive difference in its community that it would have had it not been hamstrung with a crippling tax burden. That lost revenue would have made a larger, more impactful difference in the hands of the responsible business owner than whatever Uncle Sam did with it.

To illustrate the point, if you were to take a company that made $1 in its first year and doubled its revenues for each year for 20 years, at the end of twenty years that company would have $1,048,576.00 in revenues. If you take that same company in those same circumstances and tax its revenues by 30% each year, at the end of twenty years that company would have $40,642.31. It's the power of compounding working against you, instead of for you.

I'm not advocating that we not pay taxes. I am, however, saying that if you want your business to succeed, employing a tax saving strategy will help. If you want your family to build wealth, employing a tax saving strategy will help. The best tax saving strategies use a series of business entities and trusts working together in unison to take advantage of different opportunities in the tax code. Detailing all the possible strategies is beyond the scope of this section, and even this book.

Consider this: the biggest threats to any business are from lawsuits, death or disability of the owner, and taxes. The only one that happens with certainty year in and year out is taxes. If you are interested in reading more about this idea, I recommend you read

The Power of Zero: How to Get to the 0% Tax Bracket and Transform Your Retirement by David McKnight.

    ii.   Maintaining the right records

When it comes to tax, being too aggressive with expenses can lead to penalties and interest if you're wrong, but under reporting income can lead to prison time. In other words, be as aggressive with expenses as you feel comfortable with, but never ever under report income.

Maintaining the right records is the key to making it through any audit, and even if you're never audited, maintaining accurate and organized records goes a long way in helping your business be a valuable saleable asset and make it through the due diligence of a business sale.

Whether you keep them in paper form or scan them electronically, these are the most important records to keep: bank statements, credit card statements, receipts, invoices you paid, invoices you sent to clients, copies of checks you wrote, copies of checks you deposited, copies of cash deposit slips, and past tax returns.

    iii.   What to do if you're audited

These days, most audits are conducted by letter asking for documentation regarding some specific aspect of a tax return for a particular year. That makes them no less terrifying. The other kind of audit is a comprehensive, in person audit. Those audits may cover entire tax returns, for multiple years, and for multiple businesses.

If you're ever audited, the first thing to do is respond. If you are sent the notice and you ignore it, things will only get worse. With the IRS, specifically, a lack of response can lead to tax assessments that are not challengeable, even if you could prove that you should not have been taxed if you had responded in time. You could end up owing a lot of money that you shouldn't by not responding.

When you're dealing with anyone from the IRS or Minnesota Department of Revenue, please be polite. The person you're dealing with has very broad discretion in handling your audit and can go easy or throw the book at you. If you're a jerk, which do you think they're more likely to do?

Pull together your records as best you can and have them ready to turn over, or to scan into their system if they make that an option. If you have worked with a CPA on that tax return, notify them right away about the audit. Depending on the nature of the audit, you may or may not want to have them represent you. Audit defense can be expensive and some CPAs do it well, while others don't.

The auditor will take your records, pour through them, get back to you with follow-up questions if they have any, and then make a determination about your case.

Believe it or not, some audits end favorably for the tax payer. I know someone who was audited, and was very polite to the auditor, provided all the records she had, and it turned out that the auditor found where she had overpaid on her taxes because she had failed to take some qualified business expenses that she could have within her records. Her audit lasted two days and the IRS issued her a refund.

I also know someone who got crosswise with an IRS auditor and who after four years of providing records is still in a tangle with them. Don't get crosswise with your auditor.

Chapter 14: The escape plan (it's never too early to start your exit planning)

Most business owners put a significant amount of time and money into growing their businesses, and expect to get something for all that effort at some point in the future. For many business owners, their own business is where they expect the source of their retirement funds to come from. In other words, there are plenty of small business owners who have not diversified their portfolios.

It's never too late to start planning your exit. In fact, the most successful business people start with the end in mind. That way, they build the business in a way that supports that end and they don't have to take heroic measures to get the business ready when they're ready to retire or sell it.

Also, when business owners build their business with the end in mind, they are in a better position if something happens to them and they can no longer run the business. Most of the time, a business will go under or sell at a significant discount if an owner unexpectedly dies or gets too sick to run the business and there's been no preparation or exit planning.

a. Getting systems and processes documented

If everything about your business is dependent on you, your business is going to have a problem if you're not involved in it. Even if everything about your business is not dependent on you, but the knowledge of how to run your business and the process of making decisions is in your head and nowhere else, your business is going to have a problem if you're not involved in it.

If you have to be involved in the business for it to work efficiently, you don't have a business that can be transferred; you have a job. Don't get me wrong, there's nothing wrong with having a business that gives you a job. But if you want your business to have some longevity past you, then you're going to need to take some steps so that the business can run efficiently without you.

Many times, businesses have systems and processes in place that are not documented. When those systems and processes aren't written down, then the only way for someone to step in and work the business is to be trained by observing how things are done, asking questions, and trying things out. This is a very inefficient way of bringing someone on board.

Most of the time in businesses with undocumented systems and processes, each person approaches the systems and processes with a little bit different set of ideas, and policies and procedures can vary widely so the business can experience inconsistent performance.

If you want your business to be a valuable saleable asset, worthy of outliving you, then you need to have your systems, processes, policies, and procedures written down. Even if you're not thinking about selling your business anytime soon, or even at all, you and your business will benefit from getting those things documented.

For one, it will be easier to get new hires up to speed. For another, it will allow you to actually take a vacation. For many business owners, taking a vacation is a great idea, but an almost unheard-of proposition in reality.

If you really want your business to have value, then also document those things that relate to your business philosophy about serving customers, creating the culture in your company, and your business' intended impact on the community. Those are the things that make your business special and having those things articulated will help someone else be able to make important decisions in alignment with those values.

b. How businesses are valued

A small business requires some care when calculating its valuation because, unlike with publicly traded businesses, it can be difficult to truly ascertain the market worth for each share. The best strategy is to turn to a professional who is specifically trained in valuing closely held companies. Some of the credentials you may want to look for are:

- ABV – Accredited in Business Valuation
- CBA – Certified Business Appraiser
- ASA – Accredited Senior Appraiser
- CVA – Certified Valuation Analyst

The value of the business may be defined in terms of the fair market value (what someone is willing to pay on the open market), the fair value (the value without certain discounts taken out), and the investment value (the value of the business to a specific, often strategic, buyer). For federal estate and gift tax, a closely held business interest is valued on its fair market value.

How the IRS evaluates businesses shapes much of how private industry also evaluates businesses. The IRS standard lists the following factors to consider when determining the fair market value for a closely held company:

a. The nature of the business and the history of the enterprise from its inception.
b. The economic outlook in general and the condition and outlook of the specific industry in particular.
c. The book value of the stock and the financial condition of the business.
d. The earning capacity of the company.
e. The dividend-paying capacity.
f. Whether or not the enterprise has goodwill (value from customer loyalty) or other intangible value.

g. Sales of the stock and the size of the block of stock to be valued.

h. The market price of stocks of corporations engaged in the same or similar line of business having their stocks actively traded in a free and open market, either on an exchange or over-the-counter.

The fair market value of closely held companies is discounted because a willing buyer would not pay full value for a minority interest in a business that is owned by family members. Closely held companies also often have limitations on what an owner can do with their shares, like those in buy-sell agreements, which also impact the business' valuation in relation to discounts, as well as gift and estate tax.

Businesses are valued using either a cost or asset approach (the value of the assets and liabilities), an income approach (the current or future income of the company multiplied by a certain number, depending on certain aspects of the business), or a market approach (what people pay for a share of stock for a similar company). Most often the cost/asset or the income approach is used, as the value can often be derived from the company's own financial records without looking to outside market data.

Small businesses often have certain adjustments that need to be made to get an accurate picture of the true value of the business. The most common of these "normalization adjustments" are:

- Overstated expenses (business owners using the business for personal expenses)
- Excess assets and inventory
- Unrecorded revenues
- Overvalued inventory
- Owner's perks
- Related party transactions (not at fair market rate)
- Discrepancies in accounting
- Depreciation

The professional who does the business valuation should provide you with a written report to the level that you need for your purpose. Like all professional work, the more comprehensive the report you ask for, the more the work will cost. Be sure you are clear on the outset as to the scope of work, how much it will cost, and the time frame in which you will get the report.

c. Who is going to take over the business?

Sometimes business owners have kids or grandkids who are involved in the business and who would naturally be in line to take over, but that isn't always the case. Sometimes the best people to take over business are the employees who are currently working in the business, and sometimes it makes sense to sell the business to an outsider.

i. Passing it on to the next generation

1. *Transferring it in full*

When a business is transferred to a family member, how that is treated tax wise depends on how the transfer took place. We mostly consider the impact of gift/estate taxes and capital gains taxes when we're looking at business transfers to family members.

In the case of a gift transfer of the business (like a parent giving the business to a child during the parent's lifetime), the transfer is subject to gift tax if the value is more than that year's annual exclusion, but that gift tax may not be due if the transfer is being applied towards the business owner's lifetime estate/gift exemption and is within the exemption amount.

This transfer may be helpful in reducing the Minnesota estate tax burden of the business owner because Minnesota does not include Federal taxable gifts in its estate calculation. Because it is a gift, there will be no step up in basis (the starting amount for capital gains tax calculation) and the receiver of the gift will be responsible for capital gains tax on the increase since the time the business owner received the business (which in the case of a start-up of a long running company, that may be a very great increase) when he or she ever sells the business.

In the case of a sale transfer of the business to a family member (like a parent to a child during the parent's lifetime), the transfer is subject to capital gains tax to the business owner, and the family member has no tax burden (except, of course, from the income or profit after they take over). Since there was a sale for value, there is a step-up in basis for the family member to the level of the cost of the purchase.

In the case of a family member receiving the business after the death of an owner as a beneficiary of their estate, the value of the business will be included in the taxable estate of the deceased business owner and any estate taxes due will be paid by the estate. The beneficiary family member will receive a step up in basis and will receive the company at the fair market value of the business.

2. *Methods for transfers with potential tax savings*

Depending on when and how the transfer takes place, there can be significant tax savings for both gift/estate taxes and capital gains taxes. Some strategies need the business to be changed into a different entity structure to work, and some strategies need a trust to be set up, but most strategies need the benefit of time to work.

a. Using Nonvoting Interest Gifts

When you have certain types of businesses, you can have the owners who are decision makers and owners who are not. When this happens, we say that the decision makers have a voting interest in the business in the owners who are not decision makers have a nonvoting interest in the business.

The nonvoting interests in a business are considered less valuable than the voting interest because the people who are not decision makers have no control over what happens with the company. For

146

the same reason, when there is an owner who has majority or controlling interest, those shares are more valuable than the shares of the minority or non-controlling owners.

Voting and nonvoting interests can be used with a general partnership, a limited partnership, a limited liability company, or a corporation (including S-corps). The advantage is that the current owner can retain control of the company while the next generation can start to get economic value, and it can allow for a gift transfer of minority interest to qualify for significant discounts on the value of the company that would not be available for a gift of controlling interest.

Incremental annual gifts under the annual gift exclusion amount can also allow for a gift tax-free transfer out of the donor's taxable estate.

iii. General Partnerships

Although general partnerships do not initially have nonvoting shares, the partners can agree through a Partnership Agreement that when any interest is transferred to another that is not admitted as a partner, that person becomes an assignee with the rights of a limited partner (nonvoting rights).

iv. Limited Partnerships

In a limited partnership, the owner may make sales or gifts of limited partnership (nonvoting) while retaining general partnership interests (voting). If the general partnership interest is small in comparison to the total interest, then the controlling interest can ultimately be transferred with a small gift or sale.

v. Limited Liability Companies

In an LLC, the financial rights and the governance rights can be separated. The Operating Agreement can be used to have two (or more) classes of membership interests, with one class having only financial rights, and the other class having both governance and financial rights.

vi. Corporations

If a current corporation does not have nonvoting shares of stock, it may recapitalize and exchange current stock for voting and nonvoting shares without triggering income tax consequences. An S-corp may only have one class of stock, so there will be only common stock, with some shares as voting shares and other shares as nonvoting shares.

b. Gifting Outright

If there is no time to execute an incremental annual gift exclusion gifting strategy, an outright gift may still provide tax savings over estate taxes upon death. The voting/nonvoting interest strategy can still be used to provide business valuation discounts and retain control, or the business can be transferred into one or more irrevocable trusts for the benefit of the next generation.

Gift tax is applied only to the value of the gift given and the tax is paid by the person giving the gift, whereas estate tax is applied to both the assets passing to the beneficiary and the assets being used to pay the tax. As long as the donor outlives his payment of gift tax by three years, the amount he or she paid is not part of the taxable estate. So, a donor that pays gift tax and outlives the payment by three years needs less money to give the same amount if given at death.

Also, gift tax is calculated based on the value of the gift when it is given. If the business is going to continue to grow in value, an earlier gift that uses some of the gift/estate tax exemption today will save exponentially more at the time of death.

If there is one business owner and he or she is making gift transfers to three or more people, then the value to the recipient is less than

148

the value to the business owner because it is a minority interest. The gifts have a lower valuation because of their minority interest status, having less impact on the total tax, as opposed to if the owner were to retain full ownership until death, and the value of the controlling interest would be part of his or her taxable estate.

Also, every gift reduces Minnesota estate taxes, even if it is potentially tax neutral for federal gift/estate tax.

c. Sales to Family Members

A sale to family members can be a relatively easy transaction and the family members can get a step-up in basis (the starting amount for capital gains tax calculation), reducing their potential capital gains liability in the future. Also, when the next generation has some personal investment, their engagement and commitment to the business tends to be higher than if the business is given to them.

 The challenges can be when family members cannot finance the purchase or when the business owner does not want to give up control. The owner who is selling has to pay capital gains tax on their gains, but that can be reduced when the sale is structured to include a consulting agreement with an annual term, which is treated as ordinary income instead of capital gains. The capital gains tax rate is often lower, but is due all at once, whereas the ordinary income rate is often higher, but will be due annually over time instead of all at once.

Something to note – if the sale is for anything less than fair market value, the IRS may treat the transaction as part sale/part gift.

d. Gift to a Grantor Retained Annuity Trust (GRAT)

I'm going to get a bit technical for this part, because there's just no other way to talk about this strategy. I'll do my best to break it down so that you won't have to go to law school to understand how it works.

At the base of the strategy is an irrevocable trust (one that cannot be changed, but that also takes the things put into it out of the estate of the person who creates the trust). The person who creates the trust is called the grantor. There's a rule with irrevocable trusts that whatever gets put into them is a gift for gift/estate tax purposes because those things are no longer available to be taxed as a part of the person's estate when they die.

Also used in this strategy is an annuity, which is a special arrangement that pays someone a specific amount every year (which you may be familiar with from a certain type of investment account or insurance). There's a rule about annuities that says the value of the annuity today (called the present value) is calculated by multiplying the annual payment amount by the "actuarial factor" for that person's current age as defined on the IRS' actuarial tables (the tables that say your likelihood of living to your next birthday.)

The present value will be less than what you ultimately would get if you were healthy and outlived the average person your age, and would be more than what you would ultimately get if you were unhealthy or had an accident and died sooner.

There's a rule that says the value of something you put into an irrevocable trust when you retain an interest in that property (like when you have a right to get paid an annual annuity) is calculated by taking the current value of the item and subtracting the present value of the retained interest (i.e. the present value of the annuity). The amount left over after subtracting the value of the retained interest is called the remainder interest.

If you put something in an irrevocable trust but retain an interest in that property with an annual annuity, the gift tax will be calculated on the remainder interest. Remember from the previous section that gift tax is calculated on the value of the gift when it is given. In this case, the value of the property is reduced by the present value of the annuity, so that amount isn't part of the gift. Only the remainder interest is taxable.

Consider this, if the present value of the annuity were more than the current market value of the property being transferred into the trust, then there would be no value in the remainder interest, so there wouldn't be anything subject to gift taxes.

The technical legal name for the trust that this strategy uses is a Grantor Retained Annuity Trust, or GRAT for short. It is an irrevocable trust in which the grantor retains an interest in the trust property with a right to an annual annuity payment.

With a Grantor Retained Annuity Trust, the grantor (you) transfers the assets (the business) to the trust and retains the right to receive annual annuity payments for a certain number of years. The amount of the annuity is usually set at the amount that there will be no present value of the remainder interest, so there will be no gift tax and it will use none of the gift/estate tax exemption. At the end of the term, the trust property transfers to the beneficiaries. Even if the business grows in value while it is in the GRAT, it can potentially pass to the next generation at no tax cost.

If you die during the annuity term, then the business goes back into your taxable estate. However, if that is a concern, a second irrevocable trust can be set up to own a term life insurance policy on your life (called an Irrevocable Life Insurance Trust, or ILIT for short) for the term of the GRAT to pay the estate taxes, provided you are in decent enough health to get the policy issued, of course.

The minimum term for a GRAT is two years. However, for a closely held company a longer term can be used so that the annuity payments can be made from the cash distributions of the business, whereas a more aggressive term may require a transfer of stock to cover the annuity payment if the business does not have enough cash flow, which partially defeats the purpose of getting the business out of your estate.

Another strategy is to fund the GRAT with a combination of the business and some liquid investments like an investment account;

the liquid investments can be used in years when the business doesn't produce enough cash flow to easily cover the annuity payments. Cash annuity payments are easy to value (it's cash, after all) as opposed to stock transfers, which would require the business to be appraised for value each time a stock transfer needed to happen.

The business can grow in value through the term of the GRAT and then pass to the beneficiaries (which can be your children, but not your grandchildren) tax free from gift or estate tax (currently at up to 40% federal, and up to 16% for Minnesota). A GRAT saves taxes on the current value of the business but creates the most tax savings in cases where the business is going to be worth more in the future than it is today.

Now, wasn't that worth slogging through all the technical explanation? Yeah baby, tax free!

e. Sale to an Irrevocable Grantor Trust

Once again, I'm going to get a bit technical, but hopefully it will be worth it. You may want the potential tax savings available from sophisticated planning like a GRAT in the previous section, but you also may want to leave your business to a grandchild, which you cannot do with a GRAT. If that is the case, you will want to consider an Irrevocable Grantor Trust.

Just like the last strategy, at the base of this strategy is an irrevocable trust (one that cannot be changed, but that also takes the things put into it out of the estate of the person who creates the trust). There's a rule with irrevocable trusts that whatever gets put into them is a gift for gift/estate tax purposes because those things are no longer available to be taxed as a part of the person's estate when they die.

There's also a rule, related to estate tax, that says that if you give taxable gifts to your grandchildren (or anyone more than 37 ½ years younger than you), you have to pay an additional generation skipping transfer tax (GST) on top of the gift tax, which essentially has you paying the equivalent of twice the gift tax. The idea is that if you gave the money to the parent, the IRS would collect a tax on it, and when the parent gave the money to the child, the IRS would collect again. You are cutting out the parent, but the IRS still wants its share of the tax that would have come from the parent.

The person who creates the trust is called the grantor. There's a rule that says that the income produced by a grantor trust (which is a trust that the grantor retains some rights in) is reported on the grantor's personal tax return at their personal tax bracket rate instead of being reported by the trust itself and paid at the trust tax rate.

There's a concept in trust planning that says you can create an irrevocable trust that is "defective" for income tax purposes (making it a grantor trust) but effective for estate tax purposes (making it not be included in the estate of the grantor). We call this an intentionally defective grantor trust. I know it's weird. Just stick with me.

Why is it important that this trust be a grantor trust? Because transactions between the grantor and the trust are disregarded for tax purposes, because they are both reported on the grantor's personal tax return. That means you can sell property (i.e. shares of your business) to the trust without paying capital gains tax.

A sale to an irrevocable grantor trust is a type of intentionally defective grantor trust where you set up an irrevocable trust with some "seed money" (usually 10-20% of the value of your business), and then sell the business to the trust with a promissory note (the trust owes you money over time, and you have essentially sold your company to the trust with seller financing). The promissory note has flexible terms, allowing the payments to be amortized over the term of the note, or interest only paid with a balloon payment at the end of the term.

The business' value for the purpose of your estate is frozen at the sale value, while it can continue to appreciate rapidly in the trust. If you die before the term ends, the promissory note is part of your estate but the business transfers to your family members free of tax.

A drawback to an irrevocable grantor trust, though, is that it requires an independent trustee (unlike with a GRAT, where you can be the trustee), so you need to be ready to give up some control. It doesn't mean that you have to give up control of running your company, though. You can be an officer of the company, making executive decisions, while the company is owned by your trust, which is administered by the trustee. It could happen, though, that the trustee could disapprove of how you were running the company and replace you, if needed.

The trust is a grantor trust for income tax purposes, so you are treated as the owner and the trust can own any kind of stock that you can own (including S-corp stock). As a grantor trust, you do not pay capital gains tax on the sale to the trust, and the trust does not get to take an interest deduction on the interest it pays on the note, and you do not recognize any interest income.

Essentially, you are selling to yourself, and borrowing from yourself, and paying interest to yourself. The trust retains your basis in the assets (the starting value used for capital gains tax), and not a cost basis based on the purchase price.

You will be taxed on all of the income of the trust and any capital gains if the assets are sold, as though you still owned them outright, even though you may not get any of the income or gain. Although you are paying income tax for income you are not receiving, you are allowed to reduce the size of your taxable estate while making a tax-free gift of your business to the next generation (or even a skipped generation, your grandchildren).

While a sale to an irrevocable grantor trust is similar in many respects to a GRAT, it is better in instances where the distributions

154

from the business are not consistent year after year (and so it may be hard to make annuity payments) and if you want to transfer the business to a grandchild (which a GRAT cannot do).

f.   Self-Cancelling Installment Notes

For any transaction involving a loan (including a sale to family members or to an irrevocable grantor trust), a self-cancelling installment note (SCIN) provides that the note will be cancelled if the lender (you) dies before the note term ends.

By the IRS' rules, the term of the note may not exceed the life expectancy of the lender, so your health and life expectancy are important factors to consider. There must be a risk premium of either a higher interest rate or a higher purchase price amount. If you do not die during the term of the note, then the tax savings is taken up by the increased risk premium paid over time. If you do die during the term of the note, there is a significant tax savings.

A SCIN is a good tool to use when your health indicates that you will not live as long as expected on the actuarial table, but your health is not so bad as to be considered terminally ill or have the IRS use your actual life expectancy rather than the actuarial tables.

ii.   Passing it on to your key people

Sometimes business owners don't have family they want to leave the business to (or who want to take over the business), and don't want to go through the hassle of preparing the business to sell (either the sale price wouldn't make the effort be worth it or they have all the money they need and are ready to walk away). They may still want to have the business continue, though, to be able to provide for the people who work for them.

In those cases, a transfer to key employees is often the perfect solution. The transfer may be a heavily discounted sale with installment payments, so that the employees can afford the transaction, or it may be a gift (which if given to enough people, can be done without triggering a gift tax), or it may be some incremental transfer over time in the form of an earn out.

The benefit to you, the business owner, is that the key employees already know what they are doing; you don't have to worry about whether or not they can succeed.

iii.   Selling your business

Not every business owner has children or grandchildren who want to take over the business. At the same time, many business owners have a large portion of their net worth tied up in their companies. At some point, these business owners are going to want to sell the business and retire.

There are plenty of factors that go into preparing a business for a profitable sale, and the work that goes into getting the business, and the business owner, ready is beyond the scope of this book. If you want to know more about that subject, I recommend you read *How to Sell your Business for More Than its Worth* by Michelle Seiler-Tucker. At the moment, what you need to know is that businesses are often unsaleable, or will sell at a heavily discounted rate, when the proper foundation has not been laid to make the business an attractive asset to potential buyers.

You may want to get help from a good business consultant who specializes in getting businesses ready to sell, and I recommend you do that sooner than later. Some things take time to get the business in the best position for selling, and if you start your preparation too late, you won't be able to maximize what you will get for your business.

Even if you think that selling the business would be far off on the horizon, doing the things that make your business a valuable saleable asset gives you a safety net so that if something were to happen to you, the business could be sold for value instead of imploding with no monetary reward for you or your family.

1. Business Structure Conversion

According to the Small Business Administration, over 70% of businesses in the U.S. are sole proprietorships, meaning they have no separate corporate entity structure independent of its owner. When it comes time to sell a business, few business buyers are interested in buying a sole proprietorship, mainly because there is no business liability protection in that structure.

Even if there will not be a sale to an independent buyer in an arm's length transaction, divvying up interest in a sole proprietorship among multiple new owners is difficult to do, and harder still to document well unless everyone is willing to come together to execute a partnership agreement. When it comes time to transfer ownership, many sole proprietorships get reorganized into a corporation (often an s-corp) or a limited liability corporation (LLC).

Even a business that has been an LLC may restructure as a corporation in order to be more attractive to potential buyers, as stock shares are more easily transferred than LLC membership interests.

Before you consider making the conversion, though, it is important to do a careful analysis of 1) whether the proposed conversion will be a taxable event in and of itself, 2) whether the new entity structure will cause higher tax consequences upon the business' sale, 3) how the conversion's treatment of basis (the amount that will be subject to capital gains tax) will affect the overall tax burden.

Even if there are some tax consequences, the benefits may outweigh the costs. However, it is much better knowing what those consequences will be in advance and taking them into consideration as you make the final decision on making the conversion.

It's important to note, too, that some conversions are easier to conduct than others. For instance, it is easier to convert from a partnership-taxed LLC to a corporation, but much harder to convert from a corporation to a partnership-taxed LLC and it is a taxable event.

2. *Types of business sales*

How a business sale is structured is decided by two important factors: how liability will be handled, and how taxes will be handled.

Known liabilities can be dealt with or discounted from the purchase price; unknown, undisclosed, or contingent liabilities (liabilities that will only arise if certain things happen or conditions arise), however, are another matter. Not all liabilities are easily known at the time of a business sale, and while seller indemnification (a promise to reimburse the buyer if a liability arises) should help alleviate potential liability, often sellers are not in a financial position to fully indemnify the buyer. For this reason, buyers often want to structure business sales in a way that will automatically limit their liability.

Business sales come in three basic forms: an asset purchase, a stock purchase, and a merger, plus in Minnesota there is also the plan of exchange, which is something like a stock purchase and merger hybrid.

- Asset purchase – the buyer buys the assets of the company and specifies which, if any, liabilities he or she is willing to assume. The seller is responsible for all other unknown, undisclosed, or contingent liabilities.

- Stock purchase – if all of the stock is acquired, all of the business' liabilities are also acquired. (But, if the seller will be a subsidiary of the buyer, then the liabilities are limited to the investment in the seller's company and anything buyer put into that company)

- Merger – if the buyer merges directly with the seller, all of the seller's liabilities will be assumed by the buyer. (But, if the seller will be a subsidiary of the buyer, then the liabilities are limited to the investment in the seller's company and anything buyer put into that company)

Under federal law, environmental liability (from things like chemical contamination) can follow the assets in an asset purchase, so liability limitation is not always guaranteed.

3. *Common elements of business sales*

Some common elements in business sales, in addition to the type of sale, include:

a. Seller Financing or Deferred Payments

Often the full purchase price is not paid at closing, instead the buyer makes a down payment and the seller accepts a promissory note. Payments will be made over time and there will be contractual provisions in case of default.

b. Security for the Seller

When part of the payments is deferred, the seller may require some sort of security or collateral to secure the promissory note.

c. Security for the Buyer

There is almost always some indemnification (promise to reimburse in case of liability) provision that protects the buyer for a breach of the purchase agreement or the representations about the business the seller made during the sale process. Buyers often require some security from the seller, usually some amount of money held in escrow for a specific time period or the right to off-set on deferred payments. In larger transactions, there is a smaller amount set aside in an escrow account and the seller relies on a special "representations and warranties" insurance policy for the rest.

d. Contingent Price

A portion of the sales price may be contingent on the business performing at certain metrics after the purchase.

e. Leveraging the Purchase

Some of the purchase may be funded by the buyer borrowing against the assets of the company, meaning that the company will have more debt after the purchase then it had before the purchase, but the buyer didn't need to bring as much of his or her own money to buy the business.

4. *Business sale tax considerations*

Before we get into the business sale tax considerations, I have to give a bit of a warning. Business sales are subject to some crazy complicated tax rules and it is not wise to make business sale decisions without getting qualified tax advice. By qualified tax advice, I do not mean the guy at H&R Block that does your personal taxes. I mean a business specialist CPA who advises on a dozen or so business sales each year (not a dabbler). The difference in getting qualified advice and not getting qualified advice can mean the difference in you taking home the majority of the sale proceeds or you sending the majority of the sale proceeds to Uncle Sam.

The time to get the qualified tax advice is before you start the sales process. If you know the tax implications of the various sales types available to you, you can pick the one that is most advantageous to you and offer your business for sale strictly under that sale type. If you find a buyer and then start looking at how to structure the deal, it may be too late; the buyer will likely take negotiating the type of sale transaction as part of negotiating the sale itself, and you may end up in a position to take concessions that have bad tax consequences just to get the deal done. If you don't consider the tax implications of the sale at all, and just do the sale however it happens, you may be in for a very unpleasant surprise right around April 15th.

a.   Transfer Taxes

Real estate transfers and transfers of vehicles will require that transfer taxes be paid. In Minnesota, there are exceptions to the sales and use tax that will prevent the tax from applying, namely when inventory is not at the point of sale "at retail" and when substantially all the assets of a trade or business are sold.

Transfer taxes are generally not required in a stock purchase, however, since the owner of the asset (the company) is not changing.

It is useful to decide in advance who will be responsible for transfer taxes, if any should apply for the assets of the transaction.

b.   Seller's Considerations

The seller's main tax considerations are minimizing the total taxes that need to be paid and managing installment reporting if the buyer is making deferred payments.

If the company is a C-corp, the seller usually does not want an asset purchase for cash because the corporation itself pays tax on the sale of the asset, and then the owner pays tax when the corporation distributes the net proceeds. Likewise, an S-corp is subject to some complicated rules regarding capital gains and depreciation allocation and in effect has the same double taxation problem. For this reason, corporation sellers prefer stock purchases.

If the business is an LLC (that is not taxed as an S-corp or C-corp), there will only be one level of taxation and the capital gains will be passed on to the members, so a seller has the same taxation whether the sale is an asset purchase or a purchase of interest.

c.   Buyer's Considerations

The buyer's main tax considerations include maximizing the deductibility of the purchase price, deciding whether to add the purchase price to the basis or not (for future capital gains purposes), preserving favorable tax attributes of the company like net loss carryovers, and getting the most favorable allocation of the price to assets that can be expensed or most quickly depreciated.

Buyers generally prefer to make asset purchases, not only for liability limitation reasons, but also because the buyer gets a step-up in basis for capital gains purposes. Not only does this reduce eventual capital gains to the buyer, but it also increases the amount that can be taken with depreciation and amortized deductions.

Buyers, however, will prefer to make a stock purchase when the basis of the company is higher than the purchase price (and thus retain the higher basis) or when there are favorable tax attributes like loss carryovers. There are limits to a buyer's use of loss carryovers, so it may be better to use an asset purchase and allow the seller to use the loss carryover to offset gains.

5.   *Aspects of preparing for the sale*

If done right, preparation can make the business sale more profitable and the transaction go more smoothly. If done poorly or not at all, lack of effective preparation can make the business sale process painful for everyone involved and can even kill the deal. If you start the sale process and the deal is called off, the other potential buyers may or may not be willing to take a second look at your company; and if they do they will likely be looking for what problems arose that killed the previous deal, and will be looking to get your company at a bargain. In other words, you really only have one chance to get a premium sale price for your business. Preparation is the one thing you can control that can make a difference.

a.   Preparing Employees for the Sale

It is difficult for a business owner to sell the business without managers and key employees being involved in the sale process. At the same time, it is important that you not lose employees who may fear they may lose their jobs after the sale; a well-trained staff is a valuable asset that warrants a premium price. You should negotiate agreements with key employees to continue working through the sale and transition.

The consideration (the bargained-for exchange) is a specific bonus if the employee stays and/or a specific severance if the employee is terminated by the new owner within a certain amount of time. You can make the payments before closing and gain the tax benefit or the costs of these agreements can be deducted from the sale price at closing and the buyer can make the payments to the employees to get the tax benefit.

b.   Non-Disclosure Agreement (NDA)

It is common for a seller to require that a potential buyer enter into a confidentiality and non-disclosure agreement before entering into negotiations or providing any documents or due diligence materials. It is often important that competitors, vendors, and customers not learn about a pending sale in advance, and it is also equally important that the potential buyer not be able to use the information it learned about the business to create or assist a competing business, or be able to solicit and hire away the company's employees.

c.   Letter of Intent (LOI)

Once you have determined that you may want to sell the company to a specific buyer and the buyer has determined that it wants to buy the company (provided the due diligence is favorable), you and the buyer usually draft a letter of intent, stating that you both intend to enter into an agreement and so long as that intent remains, that you will exclusively negotiate with that buyer.

d. <u>Seller's Due Diligence</u>

It is imperative for you to do some due diligence in reviewing your own company's financial statements, so that you will not be caught in a difficult negotiating position if the buyer notices something in the numbers that you have not. Any deviation of Generally Accepted Accounting Principles should be noted and explained, and eliminated if possible. You should be ready for the possibility of a working capital adjustment (the amount of cash that remains in the company's accounts at closing), so that you are prepared if the financials indicate that money will need to be added.

You should be familiar with the collectability of the account receivables, and be prepared for the buyer to negotiate a discount of that account. You should also be familiar with the inventory, and be prepared for the buyer to negotiate a discount based on excess overstock or obsolete merchandise. You should also know if accrual or reserve accounts, like reserve vacation pay for employees that have earned it, are up to date and get them up to date if they aren't. You should go through a risk analysis, and be prepared to make corrections or make concessions.

You should know your industry and marketplace, and be able to articulate your value and position in that industry and marketplace. If you cannot articulate your value, then you will not have anything to counter with when the buyer is trying to push down the sale price in negotiations.

Especially if the purchase is going to be financed, you should do due diligence on the buyer. If the buyer is not well funded without the cash flow or borrowing against the assets of the business, then mismanagement of the business once it is run by the buyer will risk their ability to make payments to you. If the buyer defaults, you may get the company back, but it will have been mismanaged, will likely have lost the most valuable employees, will likely have lost the

164

most valuable customers, and will also be leveraged (in debt) to the hilt.

In other words, you will be getting back an unsaleable business that will have to be rehabilitated. Not many owners are willing to step back in and rehabilitate a business back to the point that it will be poised for a profitable sale again. Business owners really have only one shot to sell the business, so due diligence on the buyer cannot be overlooked.

If you are working with a business broker or an investment banker, they may assist you in some aspects of your due diligence, but the responsibility is ultimately on you to get it done and be prepared.

e.   Buyer's Due Diligence

Buyer's due diligence includes a review of all the company's financials, meeting the employees, reviewing the company's contracts, assessing the company's policies and operating procedures, assessing potential liability risks, valuating the company's assets, ascertaining the strength of the company in its industry and marketplace, and doing a legal review of the company's corporate books and records.

6.   *The sales process*

If you have ever sold your house, you know that the process of selling wasn't quite as easy as just walking to the curb and putting out a for sale sign, and the process of closing wasn't quite as simple as the buyer handing you a check in exchange for the signed deed to the property. A business sale, likewise, isn't so simple either. Here is the usual process:

1.   Seller decides to sell the company.
2.   Seller prepares the company to sell.
3.   Seller gets agreements in place with employees.
4.   Seller does due diligence on company, and corrects what can be corrected.

5. Seller may market the business with a broker, investment banker, or other agent.
6. Seller and potential buyers execute non-disclosure agreements (NDAs).
7. Seller takes initial bids and sizes up buyers.
8. Seller and selected buyer execute a letter of intent (LOI).
9. Seller does due diligence on the proposed buyer while the buyer does due diligence on the seller and the company.
10. Seller and buyer negotiate the final details of the deal.
11. Seller prepares the purchase agreement and due diligence checklist.
12. Buyer reviews and provides revisions or accepts the purchase agreement.
13. The other documents (promissory note, security agreement, financing agreement, escrow agreement, transfer documents, bill of sale, etc.) are prepared.
14. The closing date is set, and the buyer and seller sign the documents on that date.

Depending on the type of business, there could be more steps, especially if real estate is involved. If the seller is a manufacturer or a business that could have an environmental impact (like a gas station, or a dry cleaner), then environmental studies often have to be done. Depending on the situation, handling the environmental aspects can derail a business sale for months, or even years.

Chapter 15: Getting the right advice from the right people (attorney, CPA, insurance agent, financial planner, business coach, and other consultants)

People usually go into business for themselves because they are very good in their technical expertise. For instance, a person who is very good at baking bread opens a bakery. What people don't always realize beforehand is that there are many, many more things to know to successfully run a business. Mostly business owners stumble along and do the best they can, learning along the way. There's nothing wrong with this approach, but it can be painful and it can delay your success. If you would prefer to have a less painful route and arrive at success more quickly, you should be seeking out the right advice from the right people.

When I say "the right advice from the right people," what I mean is expert advice from experienced people, and not opinion from someone who's never done it. When you have a business, all sorts of people will want to give you their opinion, whether or not they've ever had a business before. Listening to the opinions of people who've never run a business, and who have nothing invested in your business, is unlikely to help you succeed. Listening to the expert advice of people with experience, on the other hand, is likely to help you.

Technically, all the information you could ever want and need is available to you through books, the internet, podcasts, classes, seminars, webinars, and any other source of information out there. If information were all anyone needed, everyone would be successful. But not everyone is; so why is that? Information can only take you so far and after that you need wisdom. Wisdom comes from experience and application of information. When you get expert advice, you are tapping into wisdom.

a. When do you need to get expert advice?

Have you ever heard the adage, "When people don't know what to do, they don't do anything"? I have seen it happen time and again and I think it's true. When people ask a business owner how they're doing, business owners usually say something like "things are great," even when things are very far from great and in fact the business owner feels on the verge of panic most days.

You need to get expert advice when you're stuck, because you don't know what to do so you're not doing anything. You also need to get expert advice when you feel like you're living a double life, the "things are great" façade and the "things are far from great" reality.

b. The power of a power team

Plenty of people have alternate definitions of a power team, but my definition is the team of people who have the knowledge that you don't in areas that you need, all working together to support your success. When it is just you, you can only get as far as your knowledge, wisdom, and point of view can take you. When it is you working with disparate advisers who are not working together, you have to put all the pieces of their advice together to make it work and fill in the gaps. This is better than when it was just you, but certainly not the best that it could be. When all these people are working together in alignment, the sum is much more than the parts. You'll find that the broader range of knowledge and points of view build on each other and things happen much faster and much more easily than before.

Some people put a power team together from their peers with great success. Some people seek paid experts to put together a power team and that certainly does work, but you might not be able to afford that except in specific circumstances that warrant the investment. Whatever way you put together your power team, having one sooner than later will get you where you want to be sooner than later.

168

c. How do you choose who you work with?

You should work with people whose values align with yours. There's an abundance of people who you could work with and who would bring value to you, so why work with someone whose underlying philosophy is a mismatch to yours? I have found that other colleagues and business owners that I know who are aligned with me philosophically are connected to many more people that I don't know who are also aligned with me philosophically. When I have a need, I reach out to those people in my network and ask for a recommendation. You should likewise cultivate a diverse network of people who share your values and use that network as a filter for the best people for you to work with.

d. How much should all this cost?

"If you think it's expensive to hire a professional to do the job, wait until you hire an amateur." - Red Adair

My philosophy about the work I do is that the value to my client has to exceed the price. That is one of the reasons why I do most of the work I do on a flat fee basis, but I digress. When it comes to your business and the cost of getting any expert advice, the value to you must exceed the price. If it doesn't, either you don't see the value or you should shop around.

That said, I have worked with some very expensive business coaches that I didn't think I could afford but who made an enormous difference in my success. Of course, I saw the value and it did exceed the price, I just wasn't sure if I could afford the price. It turns out that I could afford them because of the success they helped me achieve.

Expert advice comes in a broad range of prices, and what is expensive for one person is quite affordable for another. You should get the very best advice that provides more value than the price at the level you can afford. As you go along, you may level up here and there. You may find that you outgrow some experts and not others. You may even find that one day you become the expert for someone else.

Always build into your budget the cost of getting expert advice. As you grow, that budget should also grow because you'll need advice at ever higher levels to reach the next stage. When you have the opportunity to work with someone whose success is well beyond where you are now, take that opportunity any way you can. It will be well worth it.

About the Author

I am not your typical lawyer. First of all, I don't have the mindset of the typical lawyer, and I certainly haven't had the usual career path. I came to my legal career after being a fashion designer in New York and moving away for family reasons. It's hard to be a fashion designer anywhere else, it really is.

After I became a lawyer, I started my practice and started practicing just like every other lawyer I know practices. As I was going along, I kept noticing that most law practices violate the laws of good business (and clients hate that but lawyers continue that way nonetheless). Laws of good business like providing a good experience for the client (more than just a good result), like building relationships with clients (and not just a merry-go-round of new prospects), and providing a level of care that is personalized and focused on what is important to the client (and not calling all the shots like we know what is best for you). It is amazing that law practices succeed given the usual practice model, and it is no wonder that people hate lawyers.

I don't want to be the lawyer that people hate. I want to be the lawyer that people love.

As my practice grew, I stepped further and further away from the typical law model. I stopped doing divorce work. I stopped doing whatever-came-in-the-door work. I started focusing on what I could do that made a positive difference for people, that had me enjoy my practice and my clients, and that contributed to society.

I stopped billing by the hour. I started running my law practice based on relation-ship principles. It has been a progression, and I'm constantly working to improve upon it, but I love how my law practice is now. I love my clients. I love my work. It's fun being a lawyer – the way I'm doing it.

My favorite part of what I do is working with people. I think it is a profound privilege to get to do what I do. I see things differently than most lawyers, and once people realize that about me, they really appreciate that difference.

Nonetheless, you may still want to know all about my credentials and such, so here they are. I graduated with honors from the University of Tulsa College of Law in May 2008, where I also received a certificate in Native American Law and a certificate in International and Comparative Law. I served as an editor on the Tulsa Journal of Comparative and International Law and I had a scholarly legal article published in that journal. I am licensed in Oklahoma, Minnesota, and the US District Court for the District of Minnesota.

In the past, I have served on the Board of Directors for Empowering Adults Protecting Children, a non-profit organization whose mission is to educate people how to recognize behaviors in adults that are a risk to children and intervene in non-threatening ways. I also previously served on the Advisory Board for Family Innocence, a non-profit organization whose mission is to provide an alternative to family court for families in conflict.

I currently serve as a volunteer Ambassador for Guild, Inc., a non-profit organization that serves mentally ill adults in the community. I also currently serve on the Development Committee for East Side Neighborhood Services, a non-profit human services organization that provides a wide array of services to low income individuals and families. I've been an integral part of developing the organization's legacy program and I helped implement the Elder Legal Clinic that provides pro-bono legal advice and estate planning to seniors in the community. It's some of the most rewarding work I do.

I also co-own MoreLaw Minneapolis, an executive suite exclusively for attorneys, with my mother, Sara. My office is located within that suite and I'll be delighted to give you the nickel tour if we have an appointment together. I enjoy growing that business and it's rewarding to get to help other attorneys to succeed. I love the community that we've built.

In May 2013, I was awarded a Women in Business Award by the Minneapolis St. Paul Business Journal for my work with MoreLaw Minneapolis and for my commitment to the larger Twin Cities community. In September 2016, I was awarded an Up & Coming Attorney Award by Minnesota Lawyer Magazine for my work with MoreLaw Minneapolis and the contribution it has been to the Twin Cities legal community.

Believe it or not, before going to law school, I worked as a fashion designer in New York City. And no, I don't watch Project Runway, although the one episode I did see reminded me of final exam time in my fashion design program in college. I earned my Bachelor's degree from the Fashion Institute of Technology (State University of New York) in New York City in Apparel Production Management in 1998 and I earned an Associate's degree from that same school in Fashion Design in 1995. I worked as a fashion designer in the apparel industry until I moved back to Oklahoma for family reasons.

Sometimes people ask me if I miss New York, or if I miss the fashion industry. I like New York, but I don't miss it. I love the Twin Cities and I find that the work I do now is infinitely more fulfilling to me. At the end of the day, making a difference for someone with something that is important to them is much more satisfying. I have come to understand that the path to happiness lies in serving others.

In my free time, I still enjoy creating artwork and I like exploring Minneapolis' vibrant arts community. I also love traveling and exploring new places, and I always enjoy meeting people and experiencing different cultures. I consider myself a lifetime learner, and I love to read and study topics that enrich my life and the lives of the people around me. I have the honor of being married to the most wonderful husband and sharing my life with him has been my favorite aspect of my life for these past several years.

Would you like to contact me? I'd love to hear from you.

Kimberly M. Hanlon
Lucēre Legal, LLC
310 4th Avenue South, Suite 5010
Minneapolis, Minnesota 55415
www.lucerelegal.com

www.ingramcontent.com/pod-product-compliance
Lightning Source LLC
Chambersburg PA
CBHW021803190326
41518CB00007B/423